BUILDING UTOPIA?

With all good
wishs .
    + Laurie Green
        2008

Chris Baker.
        2008.

BUILDING UTOPIA?

Seeking the authentic Church for
new communities

Edited by
LAURIE GREEN
and
CHRISTOPHER R. BAKER

First published in Great Britain in 2008

Society for Promoting Christian Knowledge
36 Causton Street
London SW1P 4ST

Unless otherwise noted, Scripture quotations are taken from the
New Revised Standard Version of the Bible, copyright © 1989 by the
Division of Christian Education of the National Council of the Churches
of Christ in the USA. Used by permission. All rights reserved.

The publisher and author acknowledge with thanks permission to
reproduce the following on p. 33:
Poem by Emma Clough, *Purfleet on Thames News*, Spring/Summer 2007.

Every effort has been made to acknowledge fully the sources of material
reproduced in this book. The publisher apologizes for any omissions that
may remain and, if notified, will ensure that full acknowledgements are
made in a subsequent edition.

British Library Cataloguing-in-Publication Data
A catalogue record for this book is available from the British Library

ISBN 978–0–281–05867–9

1 3 5 7 9 10 8 6 4 2

Typeset by Graphicraft Limited, Hong Kong
Printed in Great Britain by Ashford Colour Press

Produced on paper from sustainable forests

[I]n a world that has lost its Utopias we Christians should be a sign of hope. If this is not found among us then this is because we are afraid.

Timothy Radcliffe, What is the Point of Being a Christian? (*London: Burns and Oates, 2005, p. 69*)

Contents

Contributors

Christopher R. Baker is currently Director of Research for the William Temple Foundation, based in Manchester, where he is also a part-time Lecturer in Urban Theology at the University of Manchester. His current research interests focus on the role and identity of faith groups in civil society, especially in relation to urban regeneration and community development. He spent seven years as a theological educator in Milton Keynes, where he completed a Ph.D. on church experiences of engagement with English New Towns. His book, *The Hybrid Church in the City: Third Space Thinking*, was published in 2007.

Brian Castle has been Bishop of Tonbridge since 2002. Born and brought up in South London, he was a social worker in Lambeth and taught in Lesotho, Southern Africa, before ordination. He has been a parish priest in Southwark, Northern Zambia and Somerset, he has taught in the World Council of Churches' Ecumenical Institute at Bossey, near Geneva, and was Vice-Principal of Ripon College, Cuddesdon, Oxford. He has written on mission and the theology of hymns and in 2004 published *Unofficial God? Voices from Beyond the Walls*. He is the author of SPCK's 2009 Lent Book, *Reconciling One and All: God's Gift to the World*. He is married with three children.

Michael Fox was brought up in East London, some of the time on his father's allotment, which is now under the Thames View Estate and Barking Reach in the Thames Gateway. After reading Maths and Chemistry, Michael trained at Mirfield College before returning to the Becontree Estate as curate. All 41 years of his ministry were served in Chelmsford Diocese, successively at South Woodford, Victoria Docks, Chelmsford, Colchester and as archdeacon first in Harlow and then West Ham. A lifelong West Ham supporter, he now spends much of his time working on environmental and fair trade issues with his wife, Susan.

Laurie Green grew up in East London and studied in London and New York prior to 20 years of ministry in housing estate and inner-city parishes in Birmingham. He was principal of an ordination course for seven years and was Rector of Poplar when Canary Wharf was developed in the parish alongside abject poverty. He is Bishop of Bradwell in Chelmsford Diocese, where the Thames Estuary and M11 regeneration areas are largely situated. Among his publications are *Power to the Powerless*, *Let's Do Theology*, *Jesus and the Jubilee*, *The Impact of the Global*, and *Urban Ministry and the Kingdom of God*. He chairs the National Estate Churches Network and the Church of England's Urban Strategy Consultative Group. See <www.lauriegreen.org>

Sue Hutson has an M.A. in community development and has been involved in Christian community development work for seven years. She works for the Diocese of Southwark as Community and Parish Development Advisor. She teaches regularly, helping churches to articulate their vision of God's work in their parishes and, as a consequence, operate in ways which embrace the principles of empowerment and inclusive Christian service. She is a contributor to *Regeneration and Renewal: The Church in New and Changing Communities* (ed. Malcolm Torry, 2007).

John Perumbalath is currently Vicar of All Saints, Perry Street, and Urban Projects Officer for the Diocese of Rochester. He comes from the ancient Syrian Christian community of Kerala in southern India but was ordained a priest in the Church of North India. He was a lecturer in the New Testament at Serampore University College before he moved into parochial ministry as Vicar of St James's Church, Calcutta. His Ph.D. is in the field of biblical interpretation and his current research areas include Anglo-Catholic social vision, Benedictine spirituality and pastoral theology in urban contexts.

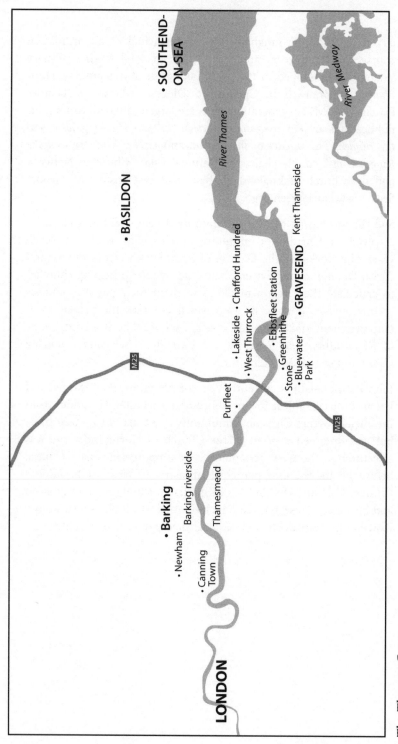

The Thames Gateway

Introduction

Britain is currently experiencing the effects of a decision by its government to build new housing on a massive scale. The targeted areas include the vast expanse of land to the north and south of the River Thames from East London all the way out to the North Sea. This is the area which has become known as the Thames Gateway, and whilst it is the main focus of this volume, the lessons we have learnt here are intended to be of service to all those living, working and ministering in similar areas of new urban development across the country. Indeed, Chapter 6 includes a description of some of these new settlements outside the south-east of England.

Other studies have sought to describe the new urban developments together with some of the projects which churches have undertaken, but we intend in this book to offer something rather different. We are concerned that whatever the Church does in response to these new urban developments, it should do it in the light of careful analysis and theological reflection. If this approach is not followed, there is a danger that the scale and dominating culture of the new urban developments may exert too much influence on our responses. It is our Christian faith which must drive our responses to these challenges, for as Christians we have an alternative perspective to bring to this new urban experience which will help us work out what building projects, mission programmes and lifestyles will be effective and proper, given the almost overwhelming challenges presented by these new urban settlements.

The process we follow in these pages is well known to urban theologians. First, it is a team exercise rather than a solitary undertaking, so that a range of perspectives is represented and the Holy Spirit may more readily inspire our imaginations. Second, we carefully look at and listen to the new situation in which we find ourselves, letting the people involved tell their own stories and offer their perspectives. Next, we attempt to analyse the experience and draw out the themes which especially demand attention. We then bring to all this the insights of our Christian faith and reflect theologically about the challenges. This active reflection creates for us new visions and springboards for mission and ministry. Describing the process in this way makes it sound more rigid than it is, and in fact the team found themselves constantly interweaving these various elements of the process each time we met. We trust that the result will be of assistance to all people of faith who seek to understand these new urban settlements as they live and minister within them.

The book is the result of a highly collaborative exercise. Ideas and suggestions arose in our discussions together and then each member of the team took on particular responsibility for the production of the drafts of one or more of the chapters, with our editors, Laurie Green and Chris Baker, taking on the task of pulling everything together and guiding us to completion. Laurie Green was responsible for writing Chapter 1. For Chapters 2 and 3, Michael Fox collected a great deal of material to offer us a description of the Gateway from the perspective of those who presently live or who will live within it. John Perumbalath undertook many interviews with urban designers, planners and developers before offering the first draft of Chapter 4, whilst Sue Hutson did the same with the fifth chapter, interviewing a wide range of public-sector employees and other care workers. Chris Baker looked further afield in Chapter 6, whilst Brian Castle drew together some of the group's theological thinking in the seventh chapter. Michael Fox and Sue Hutson worked together on Chapter 8 to describe what we found the Church doing across the Gateway, and in the final chapter Laurie Green and Chris Baker focused some of the key themes of our thinking. Laurie Green was then responsible for the final editing of the overall text.

In all this we were helped by a wider team of interviewers and cor-respondents. Among them we particularly want to thank the Revds Trish Capriello, Kenneth Clark, David Pearson, Pam Peeling, Christopher Stone, Dave Wade and Steve Williams, together with Simon Boxall, Giles Goddard and Michael Hart. Special thanks are also due to the Revd Dr Ian Jorysz for work on document formatting and to Teresa Spencer for typing the edited scripts.

Although many of the names of our interviewees have been changed to protect their confidentiality, our sincere thanks go out to all of them for sharing their views so honestly and forthrightly. They offered us their personal thoughts and feelings about what the new urban areas mean to them and we have sought to reflect upon those contributions to see if we can discern any common narrative. We believe that we have found, and offer in these pages, a coherent message and some important warnings.

1

Postcards from Utopia

They desire a better country, that is, a heavenly one. Therefore God is not ashamed to be called their God; indeed, he has prepared a city for them. *(Hebrews 11.16)*

We always hope that future generations will be proud of what we build. But judging by what we see all around us, we must not assume that this will be the case. In this twenty-first century we are presented with challenges of epic proportion which have often derived from the Utopian dreams of our forebears. They created a world which they thought would result in contentment but, instead, we find that their dreams can now so easily culminate in human tragedy. Their quest to eradicate disease and poverty now presents us with new issues relating to genetic and social engineering. The industrial revolution of which they were so proud now leaves us with the challenges of global warming and the obscene waste of ever-increasing production. As each generation of humanity searches for its Utopia it stands a good chance of creating along the way forces which themselves begin to undermine their own best-laid plans. But it is the human way to grasp after our Utopias. We insatiably desire 'a better country, a heavenly one'.

As the new millennium gets under way we find ourselves confronted by two significant markers of our new globalizing era, namely urbanization and the dominance of the market-place, each challenging our generation to respond in ways which will not mar the lives of future generations but allow them to experience human flourishing and well-being. Globalization has brought with it, first, international flows of finance and the domination of market-place relationships, and second, international flows of population resulting in intensive urbanization; and both are held up by some as signs of Utopia – the New Age of a liberal and well-provisioned future. That great driver of our new wealth, the market-place, is now dominant in every avenue of our lives, in that where decisions were once taken on the basis of the welfare and happiness of human beings, they are now so often finance-driven or else made under the persuasive influence of the illusions of the advertising industry. Personal choice in the market-place of possibilities and the urge to commodify (to make something into a saleable item for a price) seeps into our decisions about education, health, family and vocation. That second significant marker of our age, inexorable urbanization, sees populations move from rural living into towns and cities at a speed unknown thus far in human history. Every year we are witnessing as many as 30 million people moving from the countryside into the cities – that's the equivalent of the population of Spain. Indeed, the fastest-growing city in the world at present is calculated to be Lagos, which is adding 58 people every hour (Burdett and Sudjic 2008). People go where they hope to find better life-chances: opportunities for better jobs, health, education and accommodation. Many will even follow the path of investment capital across the globe, so that today, in a city like London, we find that as many as half the population were not born there at all. Urbanization and the market-place of globalization are so intrinsically linked that here in the UK, where the two are so aggressively intertwined, we must not be surprised to learn that, of all the retail space in Europe, no less than one third is to be found on our own soil. But this is only one telling example of the frightening speed of urbanization we are witnessing across the globe, with new cities rising daily in China and the Middle East and the development of housing, retail and commercial sites all across the south of England.

From the earliest moments of human history, the building of human settlements has been of such import as to make it inevitably contentious. And the interplay of modern global pressures for building sites and money-making creates a dynamic vortex which sucks local need and aspiration into a muddied whirlpool of planners, architects, politicians, international financiers, pension funds and estate agents, together with the homeless, the unemployed and economic migrants from home and abroad. Within this vortex each group can find their role much changed by the new pressures. Urban politicians, for example, now find themselves turning from their traditional roles of governance and welfare provision towards those of municipal entrepreneurs, brokering deals between financiers, landowners and their election agents. Where successful deals are struck, their cities and towns can become powerful, strategic global players, at least for a time, levering in yet more investment around the honey-pot of attractive real estate. Time was when the politicians themselves controlled the purse strings and therefore called the tune, but now they have to use their powers very differently.

It has often been argued that where local or central government had the controlling hand on urban development (as with the British post-war New Town movement), a cohesive overall strategy offered the chance for development driven by human welfare rather than money. This was so different from the piecemeal operation of the present market-led regeneration, where each developer is largely left to build what they wish. However, this distinction itself must be balanced by the fact that even where independently funded developers appear to be in the driving seat, negotiations with government and planners about planning gain, infrastructural provision and the like are notoriously strident. It also has to be said that in the post-war New Town planning, when resources became limited, many a community centre, school or clinic was axed from a development. Similarly, even large-scale strategic planning does not always lead to healthy and sustainable communities, as we can see in the 'planned' urban sprawl of much of England.

So we recognize that many factors and many agents play their part in the creation of our complex human settlements today. Dreams, politics, powers, human well-being and economics are all deeply contested as we build today's human settlements, and God is most certainly concerned and active within the process. Our incarnational faith makes it essential that we engage with these very questions as people of faith so that a Christian 'Kingdom of God' perspective can inform our debate and, if possible, help to determine outcomes.

The Church, the world and the city of God

Why do we believe that the Christian Church should bring its experience, its expertise and its theology to bear upon these questions? Has it been proved that God is really concerned for such matters?

3

It is true, let us admit, that the Church of England has, until recently, had a long love affair with rural rather than urban life, but it must also be appreciated that through its history the Christian Church at large has been predominantly urban. It began in the city of Jerusalem and its initial mode of missionary expansion was to establish itself in the cities of the Roman Empire – Corinth, Ephesus, Athens, Rome and so on – and outward from those urban bases into the surrounding city regions. Its spiritual visionaries have so often expressed their theology in urban terms – Augustine began writing his *City of God* as early as 413, while John Bunyan saw the culmination of his *Pilgrim's Progress* (1678, 1684) in the Celestial City. Indeed, as is often observed, the narrative of the Holy Bible itself begins in a garden and ends in a city. Perhaps, however, it is when we read in Luke 19.41 that as Jesus 'came near and saw the city, he wept over it' that we are moved to realize God's deep compassion for any city where human flourishing is neglected. Luke further tells us that as the final conflict of Jesus' ministry became more focused, so 'he set his face to go to Jerusalem' (Luke 9.51), and all the Gospels register that the final days of his life were centred upon that capital city. It was there that the ultimate expression of love would be enacted on the cross and the salvation of the world ensured. Time and again in the Bible, God uses urban settings to enact the divine programme of salvation. Jesus engages with the urban scene because it is here that the vital dynamics of his society are played out – and the same is quite evident today. It is quite right therefore that the Church as the Body of Christ should be in the urban arena seeking to act as prophet (proclaiming a vision of what humanity can and should be), as pastor (aware of the price paid by many in today's urban environments), and as citizen (with a presence in every parish, representative of the real experience of urban life at local community level).

This is why in the mid-1980s the Archbishop of Canterbury commissioned a report on British urban life which resulted in the now legendary *Faith in the City*. The Archbishop had been profoundly disturbed by the findings of the Scarman report about the horrific uprisings, or riots, that had taken place in Brixton, Birmingham, Tottenham and Bristol, and the Church was determined to play its part in analysing the problems and committing itself to action. The report amassed data describing the economic decline and social decay of what it termed the 'Urban Priority Areas'. It then challenged the Church to respond and it addressed the nation with a series of recommendations. The outcome was quite profound. The report ruffled many a political feather; it brought about a new awareness in the Church of the joys and sorrows of urban mission and ministry; it reawakened an urban vocation; and it helped to further a style of theology and analysis which took context really seriously. All theology is of course contextual, but now there was more awareness that where you were mattered to what you thought, how you acted and how you worshipped.

The *Faith in the City* report was published in 1985 and since then the world has faced the technological revolution and much besides. In 2003 the Urban Bishops' Panel of the Church of England therefore suggested to the new Archbishop, Dr Rowan Williams, that he commission a new report, *Faithful Cities*, to see what the new urban context was now teaching us about God and how God wanted the Church to act in this altogether different set of circumstances. In what ways had the urban situation changed over those twenty years?

A new urban scene?

Who could have imagined in 1985 that the Cold War would be overtaken by the so-called 'war against terrorism'? We lived then in a world still divided into East and West, and electronic technology, which has transformed our everyday lives and the physical environment in which we live, was still in its infancy. The words 'globalization' and 'branding' had not yet registered in the public consciousness, and the financial market, which in turn was to transform the very nature and meaning of trade, had yet to be deregulated. We were not aware of how the mega-cities of the Southern Hemisphere were beginning to have an impact on our own lives, nor how our new place in Europe was to introduce a move to UK regional government on the European model. We could see that British industries were being affected by new international economic pressures, but we did not foresee how much our coal, steel, automobile and agricultural communities were going to be ravaged or transformed. We could not have predicted that in 1998 Microsoft would take over from the production giant General Electric as the world's biggest company. The inner cores of our old cities were already suffering, having been stripped of their industry and population, but who could have guessed that Canning Town, the old slum district of the East End of London, would be gentrified to the extent that it is now too expensive for most of us even to rent a room there?

During this period many of the cities of northern England have suffered depopulation at the expense of an overheating South-East, which in turn struggles to cope with its resultant overcrowding and affluence. National inequalities of wealth have increased to obscene levels whilst migration patterns have changed the colour and culture of many of our cities and towns. Black and Asian immigrant Christians who have arrived in more recent years have been welcomed by the churches in a very different way from the vile manner in which their predecessors were received, and this has significantly changed the face of many of our urban congregations. The strikingly new cultural diversity of our cities has created a new cosmopolitan atmosphere and this, along with new facilities for leisure and fun, increasingly attracts the young to town and city centres, bringing both gentrification and the exciting rowdiness of the night-time 'fun city'.

Globalization comes on the back of the new electronic communications technology, which, in harness with the neo-liberal politics of the 1980s and 1990s, has allowed the market-place to be deregulated around the globe so that we have become a 24/7 people, trading and shopping through the night. And this has changed our culture and hence the very way we think about ourselves and our society. Indeed Margaret Thatcher famously questioned whether there could any longer be such a thing as society. For in this brave new world, whilst investment can magically appear in an area, it can just as suddenly depart; and sensing this, people caught up in this new culture have learnt to be just as mobile, cunningly sitting lightly to any remaining loyalty they may have to one particular locality. Short-term relationships to a locality are mirrored in marital relationships, which have been similarly reshaped to conform to the prevalent preference for 'shopping around' and 'taking it back if it doesn't suit'. Many therefore choose to live alone, families disintegrate, and we find ourselves being expected to relate to one another through competition rather than cooperation. The sacralization of the market, allowing it to become the arbiter of all our important societal negotiations and disputes, has created a people who are now more competitive and acquisitive – just as the market requires. If everything can be bought and sold – including volunteering and welfare – then we begin to judge value according to the balance sheet rather than Scripture, and the market becomes our god. This new neo-liberal ideological culture is bold and brash but nevertheless can become as subtle and seductive as any market-place advert, and therefore soon won the hearts and minds of many who in 1985 read the *Faith in the City* report and warmed to its more cooperatively based notions of a good and fair society.

Since 1985, regeneration, partnership and sustainable communities have become political buzzwords, and in 2000 the New Labour government published its Urban White Paper, *Our Towns and Cities – The Future* (DETR 2000), the first to address the urban situation in such a focused way since 1977. Many urban parishes have since been overrun and often overwhelmed by government schemes and initiatives. The new 'partnership' ethos of regeneration goes hand in hand with a burgeoning of the voluntary sector, in a new privatized social care system which increasingly expects voluntary and community groups to take on a new role as service providers for government. Urban renewal programmes have demolished and rebuilt many a housing estate. Private-sector investment has turned old wharves and docklands into fashionable new leisure centres, and urban sprawl is eating away at the countryside. Market-led change has created shopping malls which stand as the new cathedrals of consumerism, and new office buildings, hotels and colleges soar into the air in ever more bizarre and obscure shapes. The very face of our cities and towns has been changed and all this in just a few years. And while growing drug, alcohol and gun cultures frighten us, and the symbolic destruction of the World Trade Center in 2001 has inaugurated a growing distrust of fanatical religion, the Church of England has preferred to concern itself rather with matters of personal sexual ethics.

The academic world, however, has sought to rise to the challenge and over recent years urban studies has become, as never before, a major discipline in our universities and urban academies. What is more, an increasing number of those specialists are keen to share their learning and expertise with those of us who have hands-on responsibility for the urban scene. These new urbanologists have been teaching us that whereas in the past we were inclined to see the city first as a mechanism, and then as an organism with each part functioning in equilibrium with the others, these models no longer serve their purpose. The city and urban space must rather be seen as a contested space with many individuals and groups all fighting their corner. Doreen Massey, one of our leading British urbanologists, writes of the 'mixity' of cities and urban places (Massey, Allen and Pile 1999). A second major thrust of this burgeoning academic research centres around the all-important issue of power. The title of a short book by three British geographers puts the point boldly – *Cities for the Many, Not the Few*. It stakes out 'an alternative vision for urban life centred around the energies of its inhabitants and geared towards meeting social needs and developing capabilities', so that 'living together in cities is an enriching and creative experience' (Amin, Massey and Thrift 2000: 45). From its title alone, such a book is evidence that Christians have many allies in the quest to find ways of building urban settlements which encourage all to flourish and allow none to be oppressed.

A new physical environment?

In the medieval period undesirable trades and suspect elements of the population were driven outside the gates of London so that those remaining within could feel physically secure and safe from 'contamination'. However, as the city's trade continued to grow, so the skills and labour of those just outside the city were seen to be of growing importance to the well-being of the whole. In time, as the city became more contaminated by stench and overcrowding, these 'suburbs' became more populous and desirable, as long as reliable transport was to be had. Over time, the marriage between city and suburb blossomed to such an extent that, during the last two centuries, suburban living has become the aspiration of millions of urbanites. By the 1950s life's ambition for many of the bourgeoisie who staffed London's busy offices was to take the Tube home to their semi-detached idyll each evening and weekend. But this stereotypical picture has not done justice to the reality, which includes depressing monochrome settlements, urban sprawl and lack of community infrastructure. Indeed, many of the now down-at-heel suburban estates scattered across Essex to the east of London amount to little more than 'problem containers', with their high-rise flats looking more like human filing cabinets than the dream of 'homes for heroes'.

The old stereotype never did justice to the great variety and diversity of suburbs across the country. Dolores Hayden, in *Building Suburbia: Greenfields and Urban Growth, 1820–2000*, has been able to identify no less than seven different patterns of suburbia according to their distinctive building techniques, marketing strategies, architectural styles, patterns of development, and so on (Hayden 2003; see also Phelps *et al.* 2006). If we add to this their evident social diversity, then we can perfectly understand why the term 'suburbia' will mean different things to different people. However, one fact has given the term 'suburbia' some uniformity of meaning over the years, for the suburb has always been assumed to be reliant upon its parent urban centre for its employment, commerce and many of its services. But even though this has clearly been the case in the past, things are beginning to change. Indeed, even in the past many a British suburb hosted its own industrial units and other retail and employment opportunities. Many of the suburbs to the east of London, for instance, developed their own Thames-based transport and service industries. More recently still, we have observed a fierce acceleration in the decentralization of employment, due to the advent of modern technology and the de-industrialization of western economies more generally, and this has significantly undermined the meanings traditionally attached to the word 'suburbia'. This is why some urban analysts have begun to use other terms to describe what is afoot. Many suggest that as these urban developments increasingly become independent of their parent town or city, so we seem to be reaching a 'post-suburban' phase of development.

Edge cities

In 1991, the journalist Joel Garreau described the US experience of these increasingly independent post-suburban developments, calling them 'edge cities' (Garreau 1991). He counted well over 200 of these in the States. However, he adopted very tight criteria for an edge city, including that the development should be a new and distinct place, and that it should have more jobs than bedrooms and have at least five million square feet of leasable office space – the so-called 'work space of the Information Age'. Gordon MacLeod points out that the key axiom is that 'the edge city represents a relatively self-contained employment, shopping and entertainment node that, at least potentially, permits millions of contemporary Americans to live, work and consume in the same place; a concept that unequivocally differentiates it from the traditional domiciliary suburb and which thereby renders it at least *functionally* a city' (MacLeod 2004: 10). This same phenomenon is now evident in many parts of South-East Asia, for edge cities bring the benefits of a thrusting 'can do' culture and an attractive, well-educated workforce, and because they are built on greenfield sites, the new environments are not blighted by the scars of the industrial era that preceded them – a major problem for our British cities. Whether a definitive edge city will ever be seen in the UK is debatable, although some of Garreau's criteria might apply in some measure to those areas which have been designated by the UK government as its priority target areas for massive housing development – the M11 corridor, Ashford and its environs, Milton Keynes, and most of all, the Thames Gateway (Office of the Deputy Prime Minister 2003).

The edge cities have many critics. There is evidence that they attract only a particular segment of the population, thus heightening social segregation and inequality, and that they lack a true sense of community – being held together largely by a consumerist hub and a strong 24/7 business culture. In the USA, so-called 'successful' edge city churches tend to go with the flow of this dominant consumerist culture rather than oppose it with a more challenging gospel (Hsu 2006).

To some extent, however, this pro-business culture does resonate with the older, stereotypical suburban British notions of bourgeois semi-detached living. In both, one can see elements of the ideological values of personal advancement, competitive hard work and self-assured superiority. In this regard the continuity between old 'suburbia' and new 'edge city' might best be judged not by outward appearances, but rather by their inner meaning and ideological thrust. As recent British academics have observed, 'urban development at the edge of major cities continues to be invested with a reasonably common ideological content, albeit one refracted through different national institutional and political settings' (Phelps *et al.* 2006: 8). Outwardly, these new post-suburban developments, of which the US edge city is the apotheosis, may be considerably unlike the suburbs which preceded them, but are they at heart – spiritually, emotionally and intellectually – solidly 'suburban'?

Around the old cities and towns of the UK are growing up a variety of sprawling post-suburban 'exurbias' which, though not totally independent alternatives to their parent city on the US model, nevertheless do have many of the features of Garreau's edge city. One such feature is that some of our large new developments are based around substantial out-of-town shopping malls, as is the case with Bluewater at Dartford in the Thames Gateway and on Bristol's northern edge. Just as Garreau suggested, similar infrastructure is growing around our airports to allow for vast domiciliary settlements, hotels and car parks in the surrounding rural hinterlands. Some developments may not be totally geographically separated from the city but nevertheless are planned to offer a rounded package for local living – not always successfully, it must be added! Yet other areas, for all the interest that planners and politicians have taken in them, seem to be just more urban sprawl without amenities or community infrastructure.

Perhaps the British scene is better described by Lang's term, the 'edgeless city' (Lang 2003), as we see one urban form shading sometimes effortlessly and often abruptly into the next. Efforts are being made to change the face of some of the older suburban settlements, which have over time become containers for social maladies, whilst some of the New Town developments of the 1950s and 1960s, which soon plummeted socially, have more recently been injected with renewed economic viability and so now play their part in the political mainstream of the wider urban society. All this leaves us with an extremely diffuse suburban landscape of myriad forms which defies definition and categorization.

The post-suburban landscape and human values

It may be that academic geographers have overemphasized differences because of their fascination at seeing global urbanizing pressures turning our suburbs into exurban outer cities, edge cities, or even edgeless cities. But surely what is more fundamental is how human beings relate to these different expressions of the built environment. How are those human beings who envision and build these post-suburban landscapes affected? And what is the impact of these new environments upon those who lived there before the developers arrived and now see their homeland so changed? And what of those who arrive to inhabit these places? Where is the concern for the political, ideological, spiritual and physical well-being of the people who are affected by the environments we create? And are the new developments environmentally and socially sustainable, so that they become less reliant on mobility and provide opportunities for the development of trust and community? Or are they chimera constructions which benefit only those who construct them and then walk away to make money on the next exurban development? After all, who really are these developments meant to benefit? Are they primarily built to aid those who live there or to create the 'wow factor' which will attract financial investment for adjacent interests? It is to be noted that some of the high-profile developments within the Thames Gateway have a political and economic 'gravity' which attracts political interest and economic investment which the old city by itself may no longer have the 'sexiness' to entice. The 2012 Olympics site, for example, can lever in investment for the parent city and thereby prove highly lucrative. Manchester developed its Commonwealth Games site, which has done little in the long term for the common people but has given the city more political weight in the region. Entrepreneurs are attracted to the new development areas because they are the 'talk of the town' – they are good boats from which to fish, even if they don't prove to be good places in which to live.

Hopes and aspirations

Of course, it is always easier to criticize what is wrong and to describe ways in which human greed has fed off a good intention than to put matters right! Nevertheless, if there are to be new building developments on the present scale, our concerns about past failures can help us construct a more creative vision for the future.

Vision for a splendid urban future has an ancient lineage. The Old Testament City of David was more than merely a human settlement on a Palestinian hill – it became the source of a stream of spiritual awareness of the possibilities for the establishment of the Kingdom of Heaven on earth. Plato's *Republic* was a Utopian vision of a society ruled over by an elite group of philosopher-kings for which he later devised his *Laws* – directives for the just governance of such a realized vision. In 1516 Thomas More described his island *Utopia*, wherein the evils of society – poverty and misery – would be removed. In 1898 Ebenezer Howard formulated the Utopian concept of the Garden City, where the urban poor would live in well-planned homes within sustainable communities beyond a greenbelt surrounding the capital city. His vision combined the virtues of town living whilst avoiding rural isolation. It allowed families to escape the congestion and squalor of urban decay by providing large gardens and abundant public facilities that were still within a reasonably dense population structure. At the end of the Second World War the vision was taken up in earnest and remodelled by the New Town movement. Again, architects were inspired to plan for spacious and well-integrated community living in quite densely populated, self-sustaining, independent towns. When the resources failed, the reality proved to be less Utopian than the architects' drawings, but the New Towns did provide better homes, jobs and amenities. In so doing, however, the New Towns depopulated the adjacent city and towns of their skilled and qualified workers and high-investment industry. The New Towns were initially very attractive to city dwellers but in time their promise of a New Jerusalem proved to be illusory. But the quest for the Utopian dream community lives on.

Dreams of the perfect community act not only as abstract theories but as powerful, generative myths – the story of El Dorado became a myth so powerful that people were prepared to risk their lives to discover its whereabouts. Political philosophers have offered their visions and their strategies for the realization of those visions, but have soon become aware that the vision of a capitalist entrepreneur may be totally at odds with the vision of a Marxist, who in turn would be repelled at the thought of a religiously inspired, caste-based vision. We have already acknowledged that urban spaces are contested places but we must appreciate that they are contested from the outset – before anyone lays a single brick. And as various urban visions and Utopias vie for acceptance we must also face the fact that their realization can be spurned, spoilt, or manipulated from inception all the way to the building site. As the German professor Klaus Kunzmann has so eloquently put it, 'each story of regeneration begins with poetry and ends with real estate.' (Kunzmann 2004).

Different players in the development of these newly built settlements have different dreams, hopes and aspirations, and in their interaction and contestation, always in the context of what is actually possible, the developments take shape, and the results are bought and sold and inhabited. Many will see these new exurban places as their New Jerusalem, others as sites for unparalleled architectural expression, some as opportunities for financial gain, others as the last-ditch attempt to bring in investment for a economically vulnerable region, others as arenas for human community and culture-building. These new developments are hemmed about and imbued with profound human significance – and therefore with intense theological importance. All this is of concern to people of faith because this contestation is a tussle of powers, and the analysis of and involvement with good and evil powers is the stuff of theology and spirituality.

The Utopias of post-modern culture?

Even though individual human beings strive to put their own distinctive mark upon their little living space, most are forced to inhabit the results of the dreams and visions of others. It is therefore even more important to be concerned when the vision which others impose upon private and public space is tasteless and crass. Graham Ward writes of traditional urban Utopias as dreams of the city of 'eternal aspiration', whose creators reached out for eternal values and the vision of human community (Ward 2000). However, he posits, we are in transition, and are increasingly experiencing the results of a different dream – the emergence of the post-modern city of 'endless desire' where the global market makes consumption our god and where the only values are aesthetics and leisure. Urban space turns from community opportunity into theme park, superficial attraction and injunctions to purchase commodities. Sports, festivals, the commodification of local heritage, theme bars and architectural signifiers of a lost culture are the order of the day. Ward argues that our present theological and faith responses are based upon an urban context that is fast disappearing with the passing of the city of eternal aspiration, and that these new urban environments require new responses. If the Utopia of the new developments is framed around desire, he argues, then our responding mission must be to offer a Christian understanding of right desire – the desire of God for us and our desire for communion with God and so with other human beings.

But Utopian dreams are not just for theologians and social philosophers. Planners and those in the planning departments of local, regional and national government also have heartfelt dreams. In 1848, in response to rising anxiety about abysmal standards of building development and sanitation, the British Parliament began to lay the foundations for permanent statutory restrictions on the freedom of landowners to build as they pleased, and new local Boards of Health were assigned the responsibility of ensuring that new housing was of habitable quality. By 1875 local government was allowed to require minimum building standards, which naturally became the house-builders' norm – hence the large areas of uniform Victorian terraces to be seen to this day in our industrial towns and cities. By the 1950s the need for housing was so great that it became an important political issue. Harold Macmillan rose to prominence by meeting, as Britain's first housing minister, ambitious targets of 300,000 new homes a year – and this was trumped by the promise of an additional 100,000 per year in Harold Wilson's subsequent election campaign. The vision for more housing won the hearts of the electorate, but it resulted in lower building standards and that meant isolated blocks of flats, far away from decent amenities. The dreams of the New Town planners were rocked by directives to build housing on the green space they had so carefully integrated into their plans for healthy communal living. Then, in 1976, the Labour government put the dynamic Peter Shore into the chair of the Cabinet Committee on Urban Affairs and Shore immediately published his Inner Cities White Paper, *Policy for the Inner Cities* (DoE 1977), which switched investment from the New Town programmes to inner-city renewal. The New Towns inevitably suffered from the new restrictions on their development resources. The inner-city riots of later years reinforced the determination of British governments to concentrate their energies on the redevelopment of the inner cities, and in 1981 Michael Heseltine handed over for redevelopment 6,000 acres of so-called derelict land in the dockland area of East London to a new quango – the London Docklands Development Corporation (LDDC). Local council plans for social housing and industry in the area were abandoned by the new body and, since no meetings of the LDDC board were held in public until 1986, local accountability and scrutiny were largely absent. The visionary plan advanced by the LDDC would be to attract global finance to build a vast development which would be the spitting image of that created by the same developer on the West Side of Manhattan. Heseltine's 1981 letter to the Board called on them to 'go for as much visual impact as possible', adding somewhat belatedly, 'some priority will still need to be given to projects which improve facilities and services for those who are disadvantaged' (quoted in Boyle 1989: 43). Boyle suggests that the battle between different visions created the danger of 'the means becoming more important than the end – the marketing of the cities as investment opportunities becoming more important than the truth about the cities themselves. The rebuilding of the environment could bypass the very real and deep-seated problems of the people who live there' (Boyle 1989: 43). There is no doubt that the redevelopment of the London Docklands has proved a great success in terms of 'bricks and mortar' and it has proved to be a global attraction for London as a financial and commercial city, but whether it has served the poor who used to live there, or even those who have now moved in, is an altogether different question – or is it? Some argue that all do eventually gain from the wealth creation of the few. But the growing inequality of income and wealth together with the persistent poverty of much of East London's population seems to counter the theory quite emphatically, as related recently by Doreen Massey in her book on London – specifically the struggle of workers based in Canary Wharf for a living wage (Massey 2007: 137–9).

It was again Michael Heseltine who, looking east from a new office block in London's Docklands, expressed his dream of continuing the development of a linear city all the way down the river to the sea, in what he termed an 'East Thames Corridor', soon to be rebranded 'The Thames Gateway' – the arena of much of the research on which this book is based.

In 1997 Tony Blair's 'New Labour' government came to power and inaugurated a welter of 'New Deals', programmes and reports, including, as noted earlier, the first Urban White Paper since 1977 (DETR 2000). It promised to 'deliver an Urban Renaissance', and top architects and planners such as Richard Rogers were commissioned to advise on policy and delivery. The new vision was, first, to see the urban no longer as only a problem to be solved but an opportunity to be grasped; second, to target urban problems within the mainstream government budgets and policies rather than seeing them as marginal add-ons; third, to engage and invest in the long term rather than in short bursts; and finally, to do all this through partnership with private-sector money. In 2003, the Deputy Prime Minister, John Prescott, issued his report, *Sustainable Communities: Building for the Future* (ODPM 2003), which answered his pressing concern about 'a dysfunctional housing market' by promising to regenerate northern slums and build vast numbers of new houses in the South-East, where the problem was described as one of supply rather than dereliction. Four priority areas were designated for house-building and economic development – Ashford, Milton Keynes (already a town which conformed closely to Garreau's edge city criteria), the M11 corridor with Stansted Airport, and the Thames Gateway, running from Canary Wharf and Greenwich out along the Thames to the sea, both north and south of the river.

The aim and method of this book

When the Archbishop of Canterbury commissioned a new investigation into 'urban life and faith' in 2003, it was clear that the urban focus could no longer be confined to the inner city, as in the 1985 *Faith in the City* report, but had to be extended to the city at large and also to the new post-suburban developments which were appearing particularly in the south-east of England. A subgroup of the Commission was therefore asked to meet in order to think specifically about these new urban settlements. It included Susan Hutson, an adviser from the Southwark Diocese; Dr Christopher R. Baker from Manchester's William Temple Foundation; Brian Castle, a bishop from the south of the Thames Gateway; the then Archdeacon of West Ham, Michael Fox; and finally Dr Laurie Green, a bishop from the northern side of the Thames Gateway. When the group submitted its initial findings to the Commissioners, it had already noted ten major areas of concern that were prompting further research and which subsequently led to the writing of this book.

The first four concerns raised by the group were theological. First, what aspects of life in these new urban developments enable people to develop and grow as God has created them to be, and what aspects prevent this growth? Second, are our new urban areas based upon false values – and what could be the marks of a true and qualitative urban spirituality for these places? Third, what constitutes 'belonging' in these new developments when mobility rather than rootedness is of such consequence for its inhabitants? When people are so transitory, how can the deep trust which seems necessary for human community evolve? Finally, who is supposed to benefit from the development of new urban areas? This question emanated from our concern for God's poor.

Our next series of questions were more sociological. First, what is the nature of post-suburban religion and spirituality? Then, what might be the benefits of these new settlements, where might the points of social energy be located, and could these be loci for the celebration of community? Also, in the political arena, we were keen to investigate where power was concentrated in the processes of developing new suburban places – and of course how the Church might claim a place in that process. We were struck too by the question of the role and identity of local leadership in these settlements: what should citizenship and accountability be in such areas? Finally, we had already been surprised to find that those already living in these newly developed settlements were preferring, when given the option, to worship in traditional surroundings (perhaps as sanctuary from the newness all around them). Given these circumstances, how should we monitor, support or challenge the new expressions of church in new post-suburban areas? These were the major questions which emerged from our preliminary research and which prompted us to take matters further and deeper.

The next four chapters of this book therefore recount the outcome of intensive interviews with more than 60 people who are directly involved with the development and life of the new urban and suburban areas. Those who have lived there for some time, together with those who have just arrived in these localities, express their views in Chapters 2 and 3 respectively, followed in Chapter 4 by those who envisage, plan and build these new settlements. In Chapter 5, those who offer services and amenities to the areas have their say. Since all those interviewed in these chapters are concerned primarily with the Thames Gateway, we felt it important to present in Chapter 6 an overview of similar developments across the UK.

In the final three chapters we offer our own reflections on all that has gone before. We begin, in Chapter 7, with theological reflection on the spiritual search for community and belonging, which we sensed in so many of our conversations. In Chapter 8 we examine how churches and congregations in the new developments should respond to the new challenges. And in Chapter 9 we conclude by considering the question at the heart of our enquiry, namely 'What makes a good city?' – what makes for a thriving and sustainable built environment where human beings can flourish?

As may be observed, the shape of this study therefore follows the process of contextual urban theology, noting first the experience, then moving to analysis, and thereafter reflecting upon the experience and analysis in the light of our Christian faith, all this in turn leading to proposals for action and responsive mission (Green 1990). Given the diffuse and tentative nature of the terrain, we have sought instead to listen to the views of those who are getting to know the new landscape and are prepared to share their experiences and reflections with us. We have of course been careful to consult the research findings of others who are studying these new urban areas so that our mapping of the terrain conforms entirely to the evidence they have amassed. We hope to learn from all this whether these new urban areas might offer future generations sustainable and delightful places to live, where human beings can flourish in every way, or if these British versions of the edge city are taking us to the brink of a social and spiritual precipice.

References

Amin, A., Massey, D., and Thrift, N., *Cities for the Many, Not the Few.* Policy Press, Bristol, 2000 (out of print at present).

Archbishop of Canterbury's Commission on Urban Priority Areas, *Faith in the City: A Call for Action by Church and Nation.* Church House Publishing, London, 1985.

Boyle, D., *Building Futures: A Layman's Guide to the Inner City Debate.* W. H. Allen, London, 1989.

Burdett, R., and Sudjic, D., *The Endless City.* Phaidon, London, 2008.

CULF (Commission on Urban Life and Faith), *Faithful Cities: A Call for Celebration, Vision and Justice.* Church House Publishing, London; Methodist Publishing House, Peterborough, 2006.

DETR (Department of the Environment, Transport and the Regions), *Our Towns and Cities. The Future: Delivering an Urban Renaissance.* HMSO, London, 2000.

DoE (Department of the Environment), *Policy for the Inner Cities.* HMSO, London, 1977.

Evans, G., *Measure for Measure: Evaluating the Evidence of Culture's Contribution to Regeneration.* Routledge, London, 2005.

Garreau, J., *Edge City: Life on the New Frontier.* Doubleday, New York, 1991.

Green, L., *Let's Do Theology: A Pastoral Cycle Resource Book.* Continuum, London, 1990.

Hayden, D., *Building Suburbia: Greenfields and Urban Growth, 1820–2000.* Pantheon, New York, 2003.

Hsu, A. Y., *The Suburban Christian: Finding Spiritual Vitality in the Land of Plenty.* InterVarsity Press, Downers Grove, Ill., 2006.

Kunzmann, K., Keynote speech to Intereg III Mid-Term Conference, Lille; quoted in *Regeneration and Renewal*, 19 November 2004, p. 2.

Lang, R., *Edgeless Cities: Exploring the Elusive Metropolis.* Brookings Institution Press, Washington, DC, 2003.

MacLeod, G., *Privatizing the City? The Tentative Push towards Edge Urban Developments and Gated Communities in the United Kingdom.* International Centre for Regional Regeneration and Development Studies, University of Durham, Stockton, 2004.

Massey, D., *World City*, Polity Press, Cambridge, 2007.

Massey, D., Allen, J., and Pile, S. (eds), *City Worlds.* Routledge, London, 1999.

ODPM (Office of the Deputy Prime Minister), *Sustainable Communities: Building for the Future*, ODPM, Wetherby, 2003.

Phelps, N., Parsons, N., Ballas, D., and Dowling, A., *Post-Suburban Europe: Planning and Politics at the Margins of Europe's Capital Cities.* Palgrave Macmillan, Basingstoke, 2006.

Ward, G., *Cities of God.* Routledge, London, 2000.

2

The receiving community

Having indicated something of the range and style of post-suburban communities springing up in Britain, we will focus in the next two chapters on one particular area in which many of the hopes and fears for the shape of this emerging kind of living are concentrated, namely the Thames Gateway region. In this chapter we intend to let those who already live in the area, some of them for many years, speak for themselves about their perceptions of what is happening and how it feels to them. By the time we had interviewed around 30 people from different parts of the area across the range of ages and genders, it was quite apparent that there was no one dominant story but, as might have been expected from the notion of contested urban space, sharply contrasting views and perceptions depending on the interviewees' own life experience, their roots or lack of them, and the extent to which they understood themselves to be 'at home' or physical, mental or spiritual migrants.

It is important to recall something of the history of this area, which stretches down the River Thames on both sides from the old, upriver London docks, then out to Tilbury and beyond to the sea. It divides into three sub-regions – Thames Gateway London, South Essex and North Kent – which, while starting out as essentially a regeneration exercise on a whole range of brownfield sites along the river, has now morphed in the perception of many interested laypeople into a kind of linear city stretching from Stratford in East London to Southend. On both sides of the river, of course, there has been 150 years or so of migration from central London to the increasingly distant suburbs and the commuter belt which now characterizes life across this part of the South-East. Take any train into Fenchurch Street on a weekday morning, or indeed from Southend into Liverpool Street or Chatham into London Bridge, and you will see where the primary economic driver is located. The transformation of the City of London skyline, along with the extraordinary success the second time round of Canary Wharf, with the local designation 'London is moving east', gives some idea of where the hopes for a prosperous future are focused.

The London boroughs of Newham, Greenwich and Waltham Forest saw the massive spread of the capital in the latter half of the nineteenth century. The first half of the twentieth saw a spread eastward to Barking and Dagenham, Bexley and Redbridge. Much of Havering and South Essex, like North Kent, grew dramatically during the second half of the twentieth century. One man we interviewed, who went to school in Barking immediately after the war, plotted the migration of his classmates, some across the world, but many more down the railway lines east to Havering, to Brentwood, or to Southend. His school friends were simply part of much bigger patterns of migration – the Jewish community, for instance, moved out of the old East End through Forest Gate and out to Gants Hill and has now scattered further into the suburbs from Chigwell to Chelmsford. Currently the pattern is of African and Asian migration out of inner London and into these newer areas, and we discovered this to be one factor significantly affecting people's perceptions of and attitudes toward where they lived – the London Borough of Barking and Dagenham returned twelve British National Party (BNP) councillors in 2004/5.

The Thames View Estate and Barking Reach

We can now move in closer to hear what is going on in certain key areas of regeneration and new-building activity, and hear something of the impact it is having on those already living in these local and close-knit communities. The map of the Gateway on page x will help you pick out the development areas as we address them. One of the Gateway's major developments is beginning to take place on Barking Reach, a heavily contaminated area, which previously had a range of smaller industrial works near the Barking Power Station right across to Ford's Dagenham works. There are currently some 900 houses of this new development, with a further 10,000 expected to be completed by 2021 (though in this, as in so many aspects of 'regeneration', the numbers change frequently as the perceived need for more housing in the South-East rises with each new round of government estimates). The housing has been built adjacent to the existing 1950s development of the Thames View Estate. Interestingly, when the major plans were first displayed, the outer boundary of Barking Reach was left blank, as though nothing existed there, though in reality the Thames View Estate has built a considerable history for itself. Amongst other elements of its reputation is the belief that, proportionally, it has one of the largest single-parent populations in the country (*Guardian* 2003).

Our first set of reflections comes from the residents of that estate, who now see the clusters of new housing around them owner-occupied, to a significant level by African families. What fascinated us when interviewing was the extent to which concerns about the existing estate were dominant and the perceived differences in parts of it very clearly focused around the issue of immigration. So an elderly couple who live on the extreme west of the estate, in an area normally referred to as 'Tobacco Island' since all the street names are cigarette brands, don't really see themselves as part of the estate. Their reaction was,

> As you move east across the estate it gets worse. More immigrants; council tenants and people crammed into rental housing. Some of the white people are as bad as any others. Whilst this is a good neighbourhood, the rest of the estate is so bad that the shops mostly had to close, banks were robbed and others harassed. It is not a good area to go to beyond Farr Avenue eastwards.

Interestingly, the very first new houses to be built were at the very eastern end of the existing Thames View Estate!

In response to the questions, 'What do you make of the people who have come here recently? Do they belong here?', one vociferous woman in her fifties said,

> Not a lot. They have come to rip off the state and get benefits. They don't integrate, they simply lower standards. They came for a better life but live as they did back home. There are rats and mice in my flat and I never had them before. Foreign families are living below and they are subletting, but the Council can't prove it. We have enough of our own scum; we don't need to import more. This is not a black/white thing, as the Kosovan gangs run a lot of crime in the area, people trafficking drugs, cigarettes etc. The young men fled and sought asylum. They should have stayed back there to fight and sent their families, women and children, and that would have been

OK. We need rules like Australia, where if you can't prove you will be an asset, you can't come. Illegals don't belong, those born here do. I do not belong here any more. I've moved to become more middle class. This area is no longer even working class. Most are idlers and benefit cheats, even the indigenous population.

The same person had a vision for what the place could become with the promised regeneration. She said,

I hope we will have nice river walks to join to the London walks, nice cafés and walkways and access to the river, but I fear we will get high-density living with poor medical facilities and schools, poor and inadequate traffic links. We have concerns about flooding, where the defences have been proved to be poor, and we expect raised water levels. What about plans for evacuation in any emergency? As for the plans of central government and councils, the only good part is the use of brownfield rather than greenbelt. They have token consultation and then ignore what residents suggest. They disregard the ideas and go ahead with their own plans. A lot of this would be unnecessary if they got a proper grip on borders and the illegal immigrants.

It has to be said that most interviewees from the estate were not as racist or as vitriolic in their response. A woman who has lived there almost 50 years said, 'It is a pretty estate and people are mostly very friendly. Crime is low. People seem to move about more in and out of the area, so it seems not such a village atmosphere as it used to be. There also seems to be more rubbish about.' However, she also said, 'In my road several people who have lived here many years and are senior citizens have moved away, because Barking is changing so much, and I myself am very likely to move to Norfolk in a couple of years' time for a better quality of life.' In response to the question, 'Will you go or will you stay and, if the latter, who do you think will move in?', another respondent said, 'We will be staying put, as we are happy with our council house, but it's multi-cultural, first-time buyers [moving in], as more and more properties are being sold.' More bluntly, another respondent simply said, 'We will stay put. Home is where the heart is but, if we did go, the greatest probability is that black people would move in, as has recently happened.' Clearly the issue of immigrants from different societies with different values is the predominant focus for all of these local white respondents, who have lived on the estate for between

12 and 50 years. Reactions differed substantially where the incomers were seen as being of a different class as well as a different race and culture.

Canning Town, Silvertown and North Woolwich

We move west nearer to central London for our next set of interviews. Canning Town is going through its third major redevelopment in the lifetime of many residents. The coming of the London Transport Jubilee Line dramatically altered the sense of it being a private land cut off from the rest of the world by the well-known 'iron bridge' into Poplar, the river Thames to the south, and the A13, which actually runs through its heart but for those who lived south of it formed a very significant boundary. Now Westminster is only 20 minutes away and many of the locals can be seen on a Sunday shopping at the Waitrose in Canary Wharf. The collapse of its own famed Rathbone Street Market is the negative side of this welcomed infrastructural investment. Here, as in neighbouring Silvertown to the south of the old Victoria Dock and in North Woolwich, the developments do not look anything like add-ons to an existing estate, but rather a dramatically new world of gated communities along the river and a supposed community in Britannia Village, where the housing association properties are squeezed between the main road and a wall which divides them from the private dockside properties. Here the reaction to new people is rather different.

The response of a 79-year-old woman who had lived in Silvertown since being married there 53 years ago is not untypical. 'All of them new places that have gone up look a bit posh, don't they dear? You've got to have a bit of brass to buy one of them. I expect it's the bloody council, who say they can build them well away from us, do you see? They should have kept the jobs going at the factories instead of putting them posh lot up.' Would she move? 'Them new lot, you see them getting on the railway at the airport. Got a bit of money them. Don't look bleeding happy though. Faces like a wet weekend. This is where I live and I can't see me moving, but I'm not a Silvertown girl. I was born in Poplar.' Though fear and suspicion was not as marked as in Barking, this, from a 66-year-old man, was not untypical:

I have lived in North Woolwich since I got married 42 years ago. My wife died seven years back. I feel comfortable here. This is where we had our three children. We bought the house a few years back from the landlord. We never dreamed of owning our own home. There's a lot of coloured people moving in. I've nothing against them and of course it's mostly coloured people that go to our church now, but I don't like all these Muslims moving in. It is threatening with what's going on in the world. In the past it was all white people. I don't think that people really mix. The kids as well are always up to no good. In my day you could give them a clip round the ear, but you can't do that now. The police will pull you in.

His expectations, like those of many, are coloured by the belief that it is money moving in:

Sometimes I think I should go and live in Kent near my daughter, and I probably will some time, but whilst I can manage I shall stay here. After all, this is where I have lived with my wife. It was our home. If I ever move, these houses fetch a good price now. Whoever buys it will have to have some money stashed away.

The North Woolwich community has been mixed ethnically for many years. This respondent, an African woman in her early fifties, had lived in North Woolwich for 24 years:

Once I am in my flat and have closed the door, I am happy. I am not really happy living here, but I make the best of it. I don't like it because it is dirty, the people do not look after their homes and their community. There is rubbish everywhere, the people are often very rude, swearing and shouting in the street. It never used to be as bad. Back home in my village people have nothing very much, but what they do have they take care of. The children do not behave like this. Here the children tell the parents what they will do, rather than the other way round. Many people do not want to work. In all the years I have lived here I have never claimed benefits; even if I could only get cleaning jobs I have worked. In the past people were more pleasant, although apart from the church I have never really mixed with other people. I am a very private person. The new homes which they are building are not very nice. They are very small. I wouldn't buy one of them, I would move out. I think the council are trying to create a mixed community. If it brings more money into the community, then it will be a good thing. Eventually I will go when the time is right. I will spend some time here in the UK and some time

in Africa. I expect that the person who buys my flat will do so because
it is convenient to get into the city, with the Docklands Light Railway
close by. The people who have come to live here are people who
have been educated and have highly paid jobs. I have a strong sense
of belonging to the church, but I'm not sure about belonging to the
community. I just keep myself to myself and get on the best I can.
I suppose my life is global really, here and back home in Africa.
Apart from church members, I do not have friends here in this community. I love the church. It is my life. I would not have achieved
the things which I have without God.

Her view was not untypical of the long-stay African and
Caribbean community, as can be seen in the comments of another
woman in her fifties who had lived in North Woolwich for 27 years,
about the changes resulting from the new folk moving in: 'They are
very nice, all the new flats they are building, but not in our reach,
far too much money. It was better here when it was under the GLC
[the Greater London Council]. Since the local council took over
and made all the decisions it went down.' Her experience over those
27 years was echoed by a number of people of a similar background
in Canning Town:

It's nice and quiet living here and I am happy. My children have
been raised here. When we first came we were one of the few black
people to live here. There's more trouble now with the children, you
never used to see them hanging around on the street. The parents
have no control of them. It was more of a community, there were
more shops and the school was here. Now they have to get on the
bus. My children used to come home for their dinner. There wasn't
any trouble, no cars burnt out and all the graffiti like now. They
need discipline. If I had enough money, I would move somewhere
a bit more open and clean. When I retire, all the kids will be settled
and I would like to spend six months here and six months in Nigeria.
I go to work, I sleep, I cook, I shop and I come to church. Yes, I suppose you could say my life is here. But my heart is in Africa.

Perhaps the best summary from the long-established community
came from an 82-year-old man who had lived in Silvertown all his
life:

This is my home. I have lived here all my life. I live a few streets
away from the street where I was born, but they pulled those houses
down, you know. It is where I belong and it's all I know. There isn't

much here any more, but I suppose that's just how it is. I've noticed that there's more and more dark people coming in and those who cover their faces from them Arab countries. If you look at other parts of London where that's happened, it's not good. It doesn't work and that's where the trouble starts. In the past we didn't have much, but life here was better. I always had a bit of money in my pocket and there was food on the table. It was probably harder for the missus, 'cos she had the kids to look after. I took as much work as I could. All these posh, new places aren't for the likes of us, for the working class. The council do what suits 'em, they always have and they always will. The only way I'll leave this place is in a box. You won't get me in no old people's home and I wouldn't live with my kids and their fancy ways. I don't really know them new lot who are moving into these posh flats, which look like bleeding Lego bricks to me. It don't bother me if they come and live here. Everyone to their own is what I say. This is my place. The kids have moved away. My brother went to live in Wales and the others are dead and gone. Never really been one to go to church, but I expect they do a lot of good for them who need it. After all, you come and see me, darlin', don't you? More than the bleedin' kids do.

Views from Canning Town north of the docks are similar. These remarks are from someone who had been in the area for 60 years:

The best thing about the area now is the transport system. The worst is the unemployment. The regeneration area has been left to run down. No police are about and you have to go out of the area to shop. In the past everyone was employed. There was a good feel about the area, with people seeming to care about their neighbours, but my fear is that what's happening now is that local people have no say about what is happening to them. My hope is for a New Canning Town, where everyone is catered for. As for who has the say, that's the developers. I am going to stay. I am hoping for a good mixture of people, but at the prices the properties will cost, I should think it will be the people that can afford them.

Interestingly, in answer to the questions, 'What do you make of the people that have come in recently? Do they belong here and do you still belong here?', the reaction was, 'It is not a case of who belongs here. It's a case of the area not being big enough to accommodate all these extra people, especially the unemployed already here', and it is true that the figures for density of redevelopment for Canning Town are absolutely astronomic (Newham Council 2007).

A younger woman in her forties, who had been in the area for just 11 years, reflected the pace of change:

> E16 still has a strong sense of community and many resources in the locality. Anti-social behaviour seems to be on the increase, from litter on the streets to gangs of youths. The area feels more tense when walking around in the late afternoon and evening, though from when I first moved here the demographic has changed completely, as many original community members have moved out. I fear that the local area will become gated communities with a majority of City workers moving in, especially if the decanted tenants decide not to come back once the regeneration is completed,

though she said, 'My family and I will stay, as I value this community and the opportunities I hope it will continue to give us. I worry that too many having no connections will take over the tenancies or control of the housing stock, with no checks, measures or controls to who they move in to the area.' When talking of those who had come recently, she said, 'A community can embrace any family or person, but I have concerns that there appear to be small communities established in the larger community based on cultural identity and I fear these are becoming insular and isolated.' It didn't need much decoding to understand her view of the changes in the community.

It is clear that for the established communities at the western end of the Gateway the pace of change, and in particular the visibility of different ethnic groups in the last ten years, has left many tense and defensive about their life in the community, with not a high degree of confidence in the changes they expect to see.

Purfleet and Chafford Hundred

So what of those communities further down the river and further out from London? Take, for example, the developments in Purfleet and on one of the new estates, 'Chafford Hundred' in Grays. But before allowing the people there to speak for themselves, let us look again at how these communities originated. We are talking now about the eastern rim of the chalk bowl on which London lies. The chalk comes to the surface to the east of London, roughly in the area where the M25 orbital motorway around London crosses the Thames on the Queen Elizabeth Bridge, or indeed dives under in the Dartford Tunnel. Look at any older large-scale map and the words which leap out at you are 'disused pit'. This is the land of Blue Circle and the other cement-makers, companies which made quarrying one of the big early-twentieth-century industries supplying the wherewithal for London to be concreted over, and, as those companies made a fortune out of digging out the chalk pits, in the last 25 years they have been making a second fortune filling them up. Initially this was with waste but now much more productively it is with the twin pillars of out-of-town shopping (Lakeside in Essex and Bluewater in Kent) and with the road network and a whole cluster of associated transport industries. With the development of the Gateway and the coming of the Channel Tunnel Rail Link, one of the really big chalk holes is now home to Ebbsfleet International Station and the others will increasingly fill up with housing.

The process has already started: one can go to Purfleet and look at one of the estates in an old quarry there. In July 2007 the local community forum was addressed one evening by the Chief Inspector from Grays on community policing policy. The meeting degenerated as anger rose, with residents of the new estate incandescent that there at the beginning of the holiday, youngsters were petrol-bombing the estate from the top of the quarry edge and what was being done about it? Those who had lived in Purfleet for many years were also up in arms with a story of youngsters who had invaded derelict land as a gang base. The fear and anger in the estate was similar to that which we have described in Silvertown and Barking.

However, there are different interpretations of common experiences: for instance this little poem, printed in the Spring/Summer 2007 edition of *Purfleet on Thames News*. One contributor, Emma Clough, writes as a tenant rep for the estate:

> I have lived and worked in Purfleet for several years and have always found it to be a good place to live. I have even moved away for a job but resigned and came back again! So it's not perfect but what area is? It is often the case that only the bad is talked about and the good gets overlooked.

She expressed her view of the area with a poem:

> Take a look around you and tell me what you see,
> A run down looking council estate that's lacking TLC?
> There's dog poo on the pavements and rubbish all around,
> Graffiti on the walls and broken glass on the ground.
>
> A reputation for being a bad place, somewhere you don't want to go.
> Well that's what other people think but this is what I know.
> I wake up to the sound of birds chirping in the trees.
> Looking out my bedroom window, there's a wealth of green to see.
>
> A change of direction and it's the river that fills my view,
> My daughter gets excited to see the boats and yachts pass through.
> Proof House out the front, the Heritage Museum out back,
> A listed building up the road, how many can boast that?
>
> We have our own post office and that's a rarity in itself –
> The owners John and Anne-Marie stock most things on their
> shelves!
> Always a smile, a friendly word, you're greeted by your name,
> I can't think of anywhere else where I could say the same.
>
> So when I take a look around me as I'm walking down the street
> I think I could do much worse than to live in Purfleet.

Those we talked to did not appear to share her upbeat assessment of life in Purfleet today. The residents have seen many of the traditional riverside industries close, including the massive Thames Board Mill, which until recently employed 3,000 people. They have seen new riverside blocks go up and plans for a new town centre. But how far are they involved? According to one of the residents we spoke to,

> Thurrock Thames Gateway has employed consultants to work on a new master plan, but for most of us it seems as though they made up their mind before actually going to local consultation. Quite a lot of us would like [the new town centre] built on the old Thames Board Mill site, but it appears that they favour an area near the existing station. Actually the man who owns the patch of land which passes for a park alongside it has got wind of it and he has now locked up the land. I expect he is hoping for a big financial kill, but to us it appears that any spare ground will be built on – and that means houses, nothing else.

Now surely out here in South Essex it would seem that the majority of incomers are white flight from East London. Not so for Purfleet, where one resident voiced a dominant local view:

> The Barratt's estate is full of Nigerians, a lot of them nurses, etc. And then the Garrison Estate is a lot of cheap rented property with increasing numbers of Eastern Europeans. Lots of Poles and for the most part they seem to be doing the low-income jobs – lorry driving and the bottom end of shop work. It's a transit camp. Nobody stays long and lots of it's down to the buy-to-rent people. We've got a lot of DHS landlords. They buy up the older cottages and then stuff as many people in them as they can and the local council doesn't appear to be able to do anything about it. It's made a lot of us very angry.

A certain weariness, not far from resignation, was perhaps more noticeable than anger at the types of change the long-established communities are seeing in Purfleet. A long-standing resident said, 'I don't know what's going to happen to employment. It's not so bad for me. I've only got two years to go to retirement. The Thames Gateway people tell us there's new jobs coming in, but I can't see it.' The Channel Tunnel Rail Link crosses the Thames into West Thurrock, east of Purfleet, and runs up through the north of the 'village', but with no plan for a station. There was certainly some feeling that an opportunity had been missed. Upgrades to the C2C railway line into London were felt to be the best one could hope for.

Moving further east into Thurrock and Grays, the major development of the last 20 years is Chafford Hundred. This extends from just to the east of the massive Lakeside Shopping Centre up to the north-western edge of Grays town itself. Attitudes in Grays to the development vary according to whether one lives up the hill in the better parts of town or along the riverside towards poorer West Thurrock. It also has to be said that it depends an awful lot on how long one has lived in Grays. Those born and bred there look back to the times before the 1960s redevelopment of the town centre, when a number of fine buildings were lost which were clearly both a focus of civic pride and part of the sense of identity of a place that used to be a much more self-contained community with a strong sense of belonging. In the opinion of one local respondent,

'The newcomer in our street has actually been here 16 years, but she's not a Grays person.' The rise of the car culture, the M25, and a bit later Lakeside, have changed all of that.

The Chafford Hundred estate, which began to be built in the late 1980s, has become both the sign of a changed Grays and the lightning rod for local grievance. In less than 20 years 5,000 homes have been constructed in the area. Significantly, the first stage of the Chafford Hundred development was three- and four-bedroom detached properties and was perceived by the poorer communities along the river as an upmarket development, which generated quite a bit of jealousy and resentment. Said one Grays resident with obvious feeling, 'Them up there are getting everything. It's given them on a plate. We've had to work for everything here.' The sense of resentment was aggravated by the closure of the one road which gave a direct link from South Stifford and West Thurrock into Chafford Hundred (Mill Lane). Now, in order to get to the new development, one has to go up through the much more salubrious parts of North Grays via the major roundabout off the new A13. Interestingly, we found the same sense of resentment at the closure of the Old London Road in Harlow to make sure that the new Church Langley development could only be accessed from one entry point off the A414, thus clearly defining its existence over against Potter Street. The woman priest who served West Thurrock for many years recalled how, when the water main failed in the local area of West Thurrock, one youngster exploded: 'It's that bloody Chafford Hundred again, Miss!' This was at a time when the ethnic minority, which might have been expected to take the blame for perceived slights, was increasing substantially in the area, yet clearly Chafford Hundred was seen as a bigger villain than the ethnic minority. (Ironically the apparently ludicrous accusation that it was the fault of Chafford Hundred was later found to be correct! The construction workers building the new housing had severed the connection accidentally.)

Later, as Chafford Hundred developed its western edge towards the station and Lakeside, initially there were a number of upmarket detached houses which attracted some of the aspiring middle class from the first part of the development who wanted to live nearer the station. Subsequently many more one-bedroom flats were built and a slightly more realistic assessment of an estate that has its own major problems is beginning to emerge. The early perception that it was all 'outsiders' moving into Chafford Hundred belied the truth that there were many who wanted to move up-market from the poorer parts of Grays and West Thurrock itself, but some of the older residents conveniently forgot this in their antipathy to those who had it 'given to them on a plate'.

Retracing our route along the A13 and then crossing the Dartford Bridge to the south of the River Thames, we find ourselves in a scenario similar to that of the developments in the South Essex area close by the bridge. There is a perception that Bluewater, south of the Thames, is an upmarket shopping centre compared to Lakeside on the north bank, and that the new estates around that part of North Kent are a class above the Essex settlements. We are not sure. What is clear, however, is a sense in the established towns that they are being overlooked, with the attention (and investment) given to the new housing. This came from a single-parent mum, unemployed and living in a council flat locally:

> There are too many people in the area due to unreasonable housing development. Richer people are moving into the new houses while our life is getting worse. I don't know about the future of social housing. I worry about the unfortunate ones like me. At the moment I still belong to the community here, but I don't know whether the change in demography will affect my attachment to the area even though I have family and friends around here.

Contrast this from an Asian male who is a senior manager in a private multinational company: 'Some good changes have made life here better, for example Fastrack and Eurostar. More money is coming into the area and making it an ideal place to live. It's an exciting place to be and getting better.' In reply to the question, 'What do you make of the people who have come in recently?', his response was typical: 'They are people from outside, mainly those working in London areas. Some of them don't seem to belong here but I hope they will make an effort. It is too early to make a judgement.' A white male 40-year-old who works part time in a local supermarket and is a social/political activist put it this way: 'They are mostly commuters to their place of work. Many only sleep here while their actual life is elsewhere.' His personal feelings about the future were revealing: 'I am not sure if I will have a place in this much-dreamt-of "better Kent Thameside". I may not be good enough for this new world.'

Finally there is, as north of the river, a sense of a 'pecking order' among the new estates. An article in the *Guardian*'s G2 section (Barkham 2007) explored two of the new estates, Waterstone Park and Ingress Park, and found this very evident. We shall have more to say about this in the next chapter.

The impact of migration and social change

We said at the beginning of this chapter that there was no one dominant story from those who have been living in the areas now receiving the new developments that will make up the patchwork we call Thames Gateway. A number of themes, however, have emerged, some to our surprise, others perhaps to be expected. First is the theme of migration. The year 2006 saw the publication of *The New East End* (Dench, Gavron and Young 2006), which revisits the inner London of *Family and Kinship in East London* (Wilmot and Young 1957), a book which gave a whole generation a fascinating insight into the experience of migration from Tower Hamlets to one of the early outer housing estates. The new book charts the changes to the East End that the intervening years have brought, with the in-migration of a number of communities, chiefly the Bangladeshis, and of course its 'gentrification' by the young white middle class, creating both class and ethnic tensions. What we discovered right through the Gateway was, first, a significant measure of racial tension, sometimes more imagined than real; second, and related to the first, that social cohesion is difficult to attain in communities where many feel themselves leftovers from a previous generation and under varying degrees of threat from incomers. None of these places has much sense of a communal identity. It is worth noting just how many of the local church communities are amongst the few neighbourhood groups which are ethnically mixed, though there remain those churches which are clearly fairly exclusive with regard to class or ethnicity.

We are not able to assess how far the workplace is a genuine locus of encounter between different ethnic identities, though we found some evidence that more recent migrants were occupying the lower-skilled and lower-paid jobs, and indeed those which were more insecure, with the major exception of health service and local authority employment. The priest who had set up the chaplaincy to Lakeside commented that she had never seen a black manager in her time there, though of course there were a large number of black security guards. Concern about the availability of work and its future is still surprisingly high in view of the low unemployment figures across the region. Some of this at least is based on the old range of fears about 'them newcomers taking our jobs', rather than on objective assessment of job and skill fit.

Whilst many long-stay residents expect to die where they are now living, it appeared to us that an increasing number are expecting to move away on retirement, some back to their country of origin, others to a new life based on the asset value of their existing house and the capacity to buy either elsewhere in the country or overseas more cheaply. The image of Essex Man selling up and buying a villa in Spain did appear to have more than a grain of truth in it, though, we suspect, a much lower proportion in the areas we were looking at than elsewhere in the country.

Conclusion: simply spectators and consumers?

Almost unanimously amongst those we interviewed was the sense that they had little power to influence changes past and present. 'They', be it planners, local authorities, London mayor Ken Livingstone or his successor, Boris Johnson, or developers, would do what 'they' wanted to do, with a nod at consultation that was felt to be no more than a tick-box exercise in an essentially undemocratic process. How far this is the negative legacy of the welfare state, where care could be organized from cradle to grave provided you let the council paint the house the colour they decided, or how far this is an excuse for personal failure to take up any citizenship role, or whether it is simply the inevitable result of a society of spectators and consumers, is a matter open for debate. We simply present what we have heard.

References

Barkham, P., 'Patrick Barkham on the Government's Plans for 3m New Homes', *Guardian*, 19 November 2007.

Dench, G., Gavron, K., and Young, M., *The New East End*. Profile, London, 2006.

Guardian, 'The Thames Gateway: here be monsters'. *Guardian*, 29 October 2003.

Newham Council, *Projections of New Homes*. *Newham's Source: Regeneration and Partnership Dept*. Newham Council, London, 2007.

Wilmot, P., and Young, M., *Family and Kinship in East London*. Routledge, London, 1957.

3

The incomers' perspective

The issue of how newcomers to the Thames Gateway feel is largely determined by two questions: 'Where are they?' and 'Who are they?' It is already clear that the places where we interviewed have very little in common save being enclosed within the Gateway boundary. Nor are all the new housing and communities located on brownfield new-build sites. In Figure 1 (p. x) you will see Basildon, Southend and the Medway towns highlighted, as well as the London, Thurrock and Dartford areas we have talked about thus far. This indicates that much of the new housing stock and most of the promised jobs are within already existing communities. For example, by the year 2012 Basildon expects to have 10,700 new homes, a population increase of around 30,000, and 11,000 new jobs, whilst a new deepwater container port is planned for Shell Haven near Tilbury, providing 16,500 of the 26,000 new jobs for the whole of Thurrock (EERA 2006). Southend is host to the new university campus as the centre of its regeneration programme, and the Medway towns will add more than 8,000 homes as part of a range of regeneration projects (DCLG 2007). Add to this the growth in outer East London in the established centres like Barking, which is expected to have 8,500 new homes, and Rainham with a further 6,500 (DCLG 2007), and you begin to get some idea of the complexity hidden within the government's overall target of 160,000 new homes and 180,000 jobs within the Gateway by 2016 (DCLG 2006).

In all of this there are two factors which make a definitive picture nearly impossible. First is the time scale involved: most of the people we interviewed complained that the goalposts seemed to change each month depending on the latest ministerial edict and government statements and predictions that rarely corresponded to what was seen on the ground. So Barking Riverside has been through almost double figures in terms of predictions of housing numbers and consequent plans projected since the inception of the development in the late 1980s. This is of course nothing new. A priest who was sent by his bishop to work at the 'new' developments proposed in the London Borough of Newham's Beckton Marshes in 1971 found that between the time of his appointment and his arrival, Peter Walker, then the Minister of State for the Environment, had suspended the Borough's plans and hired the Travers Morgan consultancy to plan the London upriver docklands redevelopment. Looking at the Beckton area in 2007, the same priest thought the development was now only about 85 per cent complete! Regeneration on the scale we are talking about is not good soil for short-term activists. Rootedness for a generation is needed to grow communities. Yet again and again we heard complaints that 'they' – the planners, local authority staff and private-sector developers – however good they were personally, changed every few years (and sometimes every few months!).

Second, we must always be mindful of the complexity of the wider, even global backdrop on which all this new development is being carried out – as touched upon in Chapter 1. And the unpredictable global context is not confined to international finance and economic shifts (though at the time of writing the 'credit crunch' brought on by sub-prime loans in the USA looks like undermining the housing market). Additionally, we must ask whether pressures on housing because of migration, especially within the European Union, will continue. Will we begin to see greater numbers of climate-change migrants? Or will a weakening economy make the proposed developments unsustainable and unnecessary for those wishing to live in the south-east of England?

Look at the figures in the first paragraph of this chapter again and then add in the extraordinary numbers for the London Borough of Newham, also within the Thames Gateway, which in December 2007 is projecting 50,200 new homes and 110,000 more people in the borough by 2020! Of course some of those are within the existing Gateway projections, but most are not. Consider the figures for Canning Town referred to in Chapter 2 (pp. 27–31). In 2007, 1,450 houses (themselves post-World War II, high-density redevelopment) began to be demolished; half were down by the end of 2007. They will be replaced by 7,600 dwellings. Add to this a host of new flats on brownfield sites which are springing up in Canning Town parish and you can understand why the present number of parishioners, which had dropped well below 10,000, is projected to rise to 36,000 by 2016. The opening up of the Jubilee Line has been a key factor in transforming a forgotten 'village' into an attractive destination for those whose livelihoods are in the heart of London.

We have to keep in mind that the new urban areas on which this book is focused are often close to old urban areas which are undergoing similar transformations and in which many of the experiences, delights and problems are the same.

South Newham and Britannia Village: a private housing perspective

So let us turn to those areas we considered in the previous chapter, but this time let us see what the newcomers make of their new homes. In the south of Newham a significant proportion of housing in, for example, Britannia Village is owned by companies operating in the financial services sector in Canary Wharf and the City generally. Here it is not uncommon for flats to empty each Friday and leave a much-diminished population for the weekend, the new residents having joined their families in their main non-Gateway homes. The contrast is stark between this privately owned dockside section of Britannia Village and the property run by East Thames and Peabody Housing Associations, where there are no dock views, and there is a wall separating most of the two tenures. The local Baptist minister estimates that one third of the private-sector housing is buy-to-let, some of it owned by companies for their employees to use as a weekday base. Even here, ten years since the opening of the Britannia Village estate, there have been significant changes in occupancy. The same minister reported that four houses near here, owned by a faceless company, had been recently converted into bedsits to accommodate new migrants, much to the chagrin of some of the more established local residents.

These comments, from one resident living in their own property in Silvertown, are typical:

> When I first came to live here three years ago the community was far more desolate, transport links were poor, although that reflected in the price of my apartment. I could not have afforded to buy this

place further into Docklands where I work. Here, the local authority housing is very run down and many of the people do not seem motivated to work. As the new builds increase on the riverside and dockside, the outlook is far brighter. Of course the DLR [the Docklands Light Railway] has made an enormous difference; I can be in work now in a fraction of the time. I intend to stay for the foreseeable future; the investment returns so far are excellent.

This man went on to say,

I very much hope there will be places where one can relax. There are absolutely no decent wine bars, no leisure facilities and the health care is appalling. I hope the developments are not left in the hands of Newham Council, they don't exactly have a proven track record for this kind of thing. I know some of the people who have moved in relatively recently, although most of us work extremely long hours. To stay on top of one's career means staying focused, otherwise you are out. I don't have friends locally but I do socialize with friends in other parts of Docklands.

Women are also concerned about the accessibility of local amenities. A young woman had this to say:

I enjoy living in Silvertown and my home is within easy walking distance of my workplace. Transport links into the West End and the City are good. Property prices have increased by at least 50 per cent since I purchased my flat . . . However, there is a severe lack of amenities. I just don't know how local people cope without things such as private health care, which I have in place. Shopping is a bit grim, although Canary Wharf is only a short distance.

Like her male counterpart she does not see herself as belonging locally:

In the past the Royal Docks was home to the working class; all that is changing now. It can be very isolating here but it doesn't really impact on me because I am at work most of the time and go home at weekends to either my or my partner's family in Surrey . . . I do not see this as our permanent home. When the time is right we will move further out, probably closer to our families. I could not imagine living here with children, it simply would not be appropriate . . . I don't really know others here very well, unless they are people who I work with. If I am honest I have a greater sense of belonging to my home place in Surrey.

Her view of the 'indigenous' population was not particularly complimentary:

> I hope that the changes will bring about change also for the social housing; most of it is an eyesore. If this were to happen the property prices would rise significantly. Theoretically it is the people who live here who should decide what happens, but in my experience through my work [as a deputy head of a secondary school], they simply are not interested. They do not attend even at the most basic level of the Community Forum to have their say.

Both the previous interviewees were owner-occupiers and British-born. The perspective changes if you are a migrant. A young man who has lived in Silvertown for the last three years says,

> I am only here on a work visa which originally was for a three-year period but has been extended for one more year. If I were to make my home in the UK permanent I would certainly be happy to stay in this area, if financially that were possible. I expect when I move on other short-term tenants will move in, as that seems to be the pattern here . . . I can't really belong because I am passing through, though whilst I am here my life is here. One of the reasons I like it is that the accommodation is good and I am able to cycle to work. Through my work [as an insurance broker] I realize that, for many people in this community, life is a struggle. There is significant poverty, that's probably always been here . . . [but] in the time that I have lived and worked here, I see a growing division between rich and poor . . . I would like to see the new developments reflect a greater mix between the social classes but I am not sure how you make that happen. In a democratic society the people should be playing a big part in the decision-making process but I am sceptical as to if it happens.

As a parting shot, and in spite of climate change, he said, 'The weather here in winter is so depressing and I believe that reflects in the community.' He was an Australian but the reaction could equally have come from migrants from Africa and Asia, who figure largely in the changes of South Newham. The most recent wave of migration from Eastern Europe is focused in Newham, more significantly in the north of the borough (witness the shop changes on the Romford Road) and in the social housing on the Beckton Estate.

We said at the beginning of this chapter that the newcomers' view depends on who and where they are. As noted in Chapter 2, many of the 'incomers' in Barking Riverside are African families moving further out from inner East London into new owner-occupied property, and that a significant proportion of the rented market is now being taken up by Eastern European migrants. For all these groups, the evidence we found suggests a greater sense of acceptance of their new environment by those who have purchased their own homes than by those (frequently more transitory) who live in rented accommodation.

We conducted two thirds of the interviews with newcomers on the old 1950s Thames View Estate, since the new development is currently relatively small. The whole of this part of Barking Riverside is effectively cut off from the rest of the borough by the A13. The new Channel Tunnel Rail Link, which does not head underground until most of the way past the estate, is nonetheless blamed by the locals for weakening the bridge which provides the only eastern access to the area. This reinforces the sense of an enclave not belonging to the rest of the London Borough of Barking and Dagenham. As a result the recent incomers feel little sense of being a part of Thames View, since they share the isolation, and in any case there is no specific community provision and no centre yet to the new development.

This is particularly ironic, since the early plans for the Britannia Village estate in the 1990s did not show any housing at all on its northern boundary. In fact there was a wish to deny the existence of the disreputable Thames View Estate and to create a completely new and separate identity. That may come, but we suspect not until both more housing and a local centre are built. One further irony is that the Thames View Estate will no longer have a view of the River Thames since the new development is between it and the river, and the focus of the new area is expected to shift towards the river, deliberately turning its back on the old council provision.

Thames View Estate: a social housing perspective

The newcomers in the area whom we interviewed were typical of recent arrivals. Half of our interviewees lived in council property, half in private rented accommodation. All of our social housing tenants were of African or Eastern European origin. Unlike some of the long-established residents we reported on in Chapter 2, the new arrivals' initial perception was of a place that would fulfil their expectations: 'It has a quiet environment – not like other areas'; 'I wanted to live in a peaceful and quiet area like this'; 'I wanted to improve my situation'. Those expectations were not always fulfilled: 'It was a lovely area; but the east end of the estate is not as good as where I was previously. Lots of neighbour troubles, and arson attack next door and the children stone the houses from the park. And now I have a troublesome tenant above me'; 'It hasn't at all matched my expectations; Dagenham is better. I moved from a friend's place there when I became a council tenant.' This last quotation came from a Nigerian woman who has cut herself off from her family back home (a reciprocal process) and feels she belongs here, but has not yet found the beautiful place she hopes this could become. She is fearful of neighbours, the place, and the future.

Yet for most it is an improvement – somewhere on the way up and 'out from noisy Hackney to a quiet and peaceful Thames View – this is my home now'. This was a particularly interesting comment from a family of Eastern European origin, as it indicated a real belief that they had arrived at where they wanted to be – not common in our explorations. The same family had a truly positive view of life on the estate: 'There are good amenities and a 24/7 bus service in operation; we do love the community as the people are helpful and there is less crime compared with where we used to live, both in Hackney and our previous country.'

The family who had the worst experience on the estate, having moved into its eastern end, were vociferous in their condemnation and, it seemed, justifiably so:

The upstairs neighbours throw rubbish, including used condoms, into our garden. I have complained to the Council but nothing happens. The woman upstairs says she is single but her husband lives with her, neither of them work, they just cause a nuisance including noises at four in the morning. I [the wife] don't want to complain too much because my papers are not in order so I could be in trouble. They should separate those of us who work from those who don't and put them in a different area. They cause most of the trouble. I can't cope with the different culture – it's so unfriendly.

47

Purfleet and Chafford Hundred

Look further down the River Thames at Purfleet and Chafford Hundred, as we did in Chapter 2, and the picture is rather different. Consider Purfleet first. We saw how many long-term residents were struck by the mix of peoples moving in – African, Asian and East European. Here are a couple of typical newcomers' reactions to their changed life.

An Asian couple moved to Purfleet in 2006 from Dagenham, where they had lived for 20 years in a house bought from their parents which they still own and rent out, keeping it as an investment for their young children. They had wanted to move out into Essex and looked across the area as far as Chelmsford, where their parents now live. They settled on Purfleet because they liked the style of house and the fact that it would be low maintenance as it was new. The view of the River Thames as they drove into Purfleet was the clincher. For them, the move has more than met their expectations:

> It has more of a community feel than Dagenham – I take the children to many local clubs. My husband works four days a week in Wanstead and I do the same in Ilford. Two days a week mum child-minds when we are both out at work. My only disappointment is that the play area in the middle of the square outside the house is out of use until the council redoes it. There was trouble caused by football so they had to close it.

When asked about neighbours the answer again was not untypical: 'Neither have children. I did speak to one before their garden fence was put up, but now I hardly see them, as they are straight out of the house and into the car.' The family now feel Purfleet is home, that it's a strong community in which they will stay, and that the local church is a great information centre.

Irena and David's story is typical. David moved to Thurrock from north London in January 2003 after the breakdown of a previous relationship. He came to Thurrock because he had friends in the area and could rent a house from one of them. He bought his present house (built in 1985) in October 2004; it serves him well as a base to commute to London. Irena is from the Ukraine. She was studying languages at university and came to London for a year. During the course, she met David and has now decided to stay in this country, currently working as a dental nurse. David and Irena have been together since April 2005 and are engaged to be married in November 2007, with a first baby expected in March 2008.

She says, 'Purfleet is a good place to live, with everything convenient provided one has a car.' With the Lakeside and indeed Bluewater on the south side of the river, local shops have been forced to close and this causes car dependency for many of the smaller new developments. Public transport is improving as the population rises but it is a long way from becoming a 'sustainable community': 'Purfleet lacks identity: if I tell friends I come from Purfleet they have no idea where it is – the quickest way to describe it is to say it's near Lakeside.' David wonders,

> Is Purfleet a village or a town? – it isn't really either. What was it before the 1980s? Probably marshland. To me the population is new, without extended families. It is attractive because it's relatively cheap to buy a house here. But it's progressing very fast – in five years it will be completely different. The downside is that commuting into London is expensive.

Their perspective of the community is of rapid change:

> A few years ago it was very English, now it's very international, with many Eastern Europeans and a large Nigerian community. There is lots of friendliness and natural warmth; decent, hardworking people – professional types. Most have small families. There don't seem to be many pensioners and not many large families – probably because there aren't many large houses. A lot of people move for a new life after divorce, etc. There are good indoor facilities for children with clubs at the church and elsewhere, but little outside like playgrounds.

They both intend to stay long term in Purfleet: 'It has a nice feeling.' The need for a larger house for a growing family would be the only constraint.

When we turn to look at Chafford Hundred, a much bigger and more mature development in a well-defined chalk-pit area, the picture changes again. But first, some reflections from the present parish priest, who sets the context for the variety of views found on the Chafford estate:

> In a place with no history people clamour to invent history and to become community leaders. Chafford was chalk quarries. Then one quarry became Lakeside Shopping Centre, another became one of

the largest nature reserves to be set in the centre of a totally urban environment, the rest of the area was landfilled and thousands of boxes were built on top of the landfill. People now live in those boxes and call them home.

He also took pains to note that,

the community has very bad infrastructure – good but full schools. It is supposed to be eco-friendly, meaning it has lots of cycle paths, but when the wildlife trust wanted a wind-powered generator, we got the not-in-my-backyard response from residents and the planning application was turned down.

The parish priest was well aware that community needs time to grow and blossom:

The videos that were shown on cable TV to advertise the development do make it look like a new Utopia. I think people are on the one hand disappointed that not everything is as good as advertised, and on the other that there are signs we are developing and maturing as a community (with church and community-based summer fairs, fun days, etc.). People generally have a very instant mindset, and get very angry that the infrastructure takes time to plan, design and build. All the new trees and shrubs are still puppy-dog size and, as they grow, it's as if we grow with them and develop our sense of history and community and roots go down.

As an indication of how new the estate still is, he adds, 'There are so few mature trees in Chafford Hundred that the couple in the new vicarage garden have preservation orders on them!' But he noted that the sense of identity of a neighborhood can be enhanced as stories about the history of the locality emerge:

Creating tradition and seeing what history we now have is fun. The discovery during building of a World War II plane and the body of a US airman from it, preserved in clay, resulted in a grave which has become a tribute to him and also Chafford's war memorial. The church organized the first Remembrance Sunday parade to it this year. It was well attended by lots of key community people, who laid poppy wreaths.

When asked what he felt must have been the intention of the developers for his area, he replied,

As far as I am aware, Chafford Hundred is the largest privately funded new estate in Europe at present. I did once ask one of the developers if he had thought about the personalities of the people who would come to live in the boxes he was making money by selling. He hadn't!

The vicar then reflected on a crucial question:

When does a place become a place? The signposts off the A13 call us Chafford Hundred. If I give my address in a store starting with my postcode, it tells them I live in Clockhouse Lane, Grays. Whenever I give my address myself, I say I live in Clockhouse Lane, Chafford Hundred. Post addressed to me like that gets to me; post sent to Clockhouse Lane, Grays gets to another bit of my road cut off by a dual carriageway. I want a sign up that says, 'Welcome to Chafford Hundred: please drive carefully through the village'. Then I will feel this place really is a place.

Two contrasting families now give their views. The husband in the first of these arrived in Thurrock 20 years ago, just before Lakeside was built. Having lived in a newly built flat in Grays for eight years with his wife, they looked for a modern, detached family home and Chafford Hundred, then just opened, fitted the bill. They bought a three-bedroom detached house which they subsequently sold, and moved to their present five-bedroom home. They choose to stay in Chafford Hundred because they like it. They say that even if the housing stock is densely built, people are civil to each other and it feels safe. They intend to stay indefinitely. The husband works in London, as do many, and for commuters housing is cheaper than in many other Essex towns at a similar distance from the city. He was a Labour councillor for three years, and having lived in the area before moving to Chafford Hundred would always say he still lives in Grays. But this is probably not true for most. His perception and local commitment are coloured by his history and we have no way of knowing whose perception of the area is most accurate. He says,

Chafford Hundred is generally populated by local Thurrock people. The sense of community is stronger on certain streets than others. There is a focus amongst mothers at the school gates with strong PTAs at the schools. The highest population density is in the late twenties, early thirties; however there is a newer phenomenon of grandparents moving to be near their children and grandchildren, such that there are now two over-fifties clubs. This diversity is good for the community. There is little social housing – too little from my point of view. However when such housing was proposed, there was a campaign against it, which was a bit brutal and brought out the unsavoury side of people.

As you would expect from someone engaged in the local political scene, he has a good overview of upcoming issues:

People feel really disappointed that we were promised a new secondary school, but when Thurrock Unitary Authority took over from Essex County Council, these plans changed to a school on a site half the size, placed on the other side of the estate. Primary schools are very good, although there is an issue over the density of the housing: schools cannot accommodate all the children who wish to attend, so there is fear and anxiety about getting children to local schools. There are too few public buildings. I would have hoped that the church would be completed by now and am disappointed that the community has not got behind its building as much as they could. I run a local community centre and it is fully booked – we need more facilities.

He acknowledges that the estate has a wildlife centre but complains that there is only one other public green space. GP service access is an issue across the whole area. Public transport is not brilliant – generally finishing at 7.30 p.m. However, many households have two cars, so ferrying teenagers around should not be an issue. But above all for him, 'the time bomb for Chafford Hundred is when children turn into teenagers in a few years' time: no facilities and no strategy'.

In contrast, a married couple with one teenage daughter still at home, who came from Islington in 1999 and who are heavily involved in the local church – indeed came to the area because the wife felt strongly that 'God was calling me to Chafford Hundred' – experience the place somewhat differently:

The community is very varied: people from all over the place – Newcastle, Manchester, Birmingham. The hardest thing is entering relationships because of this varied background. There are too many houses for the infrastructure. You are stuck if you don't have a car. There wasn't a GP at first – now there is one, and a private dentist; a vet; two Tesco Expresses; two pubs, one wine bar. All for 10 to 15,000 people.

With a background as a Baptist pastor with considerable Anglican involvement, she is naturally forceful about the long saga of a church building for the estate: 'The church should have been part of the plans from the beginning, not added on afterwards. It won't be completed till next year.' She has run several church-based groups for children and young mums. But for both these interviewees, the new estate lacks something in not yet having a 'shrine'. They both yearn for this focus, even though the reality is that plenty of Christian action has been going on throughout the history of the estate. Our local ex-councillor was particularly impressed by the work of the church-run Bar'n'bus, a travelling youth facility which comes to Chafford Hundred every Friday night.

Greenhithe and Stone

To the south of the Thames, just to the east of the southern end of the Dartford Bridge, lie Greenhithe and Stone, though the local vicar fears that Stone's identity has already been swallowed up by its neighbour. In the interviews we conducted, there was some more evidence for this, as newcomers on Stone's estates refer to themselves as being in Greenhithe. We go first to Waterstone Park, to a young working English couple, recently married, who have bought a one-bedroom flat in which they have lived for just six months. They had looked at property in Canary Wharf and found that buying in Stone cost them the equivalent of renting in Docklands. They use Greenhithe station to commute to Charing Cross.

> Living on Waterstone Park has certainly lived up to our expectations so far. We are young city professionals and the property was marketed at people like us. Actually the publicity featured a photo of a couple who could have been us. Having Ebbsfleet [the new international station shortly to be opened] near and Bluewater Shopping Centre within walking distance is almost unbelievable . . . Waterstone Park is very new – the oldest part was built just under five years ago, and the newest parts aren't even finished. It is very commuterish and all our neighbours seem to be like us. We are so new we have not really made much contact with neighbours, but we don't suppose we will, given that many are buying homes either as a temporary expedient or as an investment.

The husband has explored an online community website for residents of the development, but that is really just starting. Nevertheless they experience welcome, newness and liveliness.

Next we move to Saxon Park. This is a more established development, being 20 years old and sited in a filled-in quarry, like so many on both sides of the river. Here we listen to a couple, both originally from Zimbabwe, who have been here for some 12 months. The husband previously lived in north-west London, the wife in Gravesend. They rent a two-bedroom flat as a typical starter home. They will in time look locally to buying something bigger with a garden, perhaps older and in need of 'doing up'. However, though welcoming the arrival of the new international station, they fear it will push up prices beyond their reach. They felt, however, that the arrival of graffiti, which they had seen in their previous localities, did not bode well for Stone's future; nevertheless, for the moment all is well. Their expectations have been met in a quiet, affordable and safe neighbourhood, conveniently located and much better than the wife's previous home in Gravesend, which she felt was 'noisy, busy and not very safe – and no place to bring up a child'.

After such a negative view of Gravesend it was interesting to hear from a professional couple who had identified the town as an 'investment opportunity due to the expected high-speed rail link' and accordingly bought a small house there. When the husband moved to work in London, he opted to live in Gravesend, and since they married in 2005 they have enjoyed life in the small town, 'where people are friendly and it's easy to get to know folk'. Their time horizon is bounded by construction possibilities – 'what will be left after 2012 and the Olympics have finished?' – and the fact that by then their baby will be of primary school age. They appreciated the advantages of the area in that it was possible to afford a bigger house and garden than in London, and when the rail service was improved it would be an even quicker commute to London. They were traditional London immigrants from Ireland and Scotland, but the local church was clearly a focus of community life for them and the one thing which gave them a new sense of belonging.

Clearly, like many we have interviewed, though the present place in which they live is their 'home', it is conceived as a place of transition on their way to an unknown future. We suspect that in this couple's case, they will not be there long enough to benefit from the new high-speed link to London, but its promise will be enough for them to sell a good asset and move on.

Conclusion

The wide range of responses we have had from incomers across the Gateway reinforces the sense of a society in which people's own personal history and immediate local experience are the dominant factors in their perception of life in new urban communities. The absence of common history or 'myths to live by' is noticeable and we shall return to this in later chapters, as we consider the theological implications of what we have found and see some of the ways the Church is responding given the variety of these individual experiences.

It would seem that despite the diverse backgrounds of those recently arrived in these new urban areas, they share a common human yearning for security and for family and personal advancement. We found a predominance of transient migrants, whose real focus of life was elsewhere – either at work or in their culture and place of origin. Life seems more privatized amongst the incomers – none being happy with this, whilst others looked back quite nostalgically to a more communal lifestyle. Most complained about a lack of supportive infrastructure, especially medical and educational facilities, and just a few felt that their new home was in need of a spiritual focus. Most were contented but looked to the future for fulfilment rather than accepting the present as their final resting point.

Just as we noted in the former chapter, however, these incomers, like those who were there before them, did not feel that they had control over the environment in which they lived. We therefore went next to the developers, the planners and the politicians to see how they perceived the growth of these new urban areas.

References

DCLG (Department of Communities and Local Government), *Thames Gateway Interim Plan: Policy Framework*. Communities and Local Government Publications, Wetherby, 2006.

Building Utopia?

DCLG, *The Delivery Plan: The Thames Gateway.* Communities and Local Government Publications, Wetherby, 2007.

EERA (East of England Regional Assembly), *East of England Plan: Draft Revision to the Regional Spatial Strategy (RSS) for the East of England.* EERA, Cambridge, 2006, revised online, June 2006; available at <http://goe-consult.limehouse.co.uk/portal/rss/rss?pointid=project_827>.

4

Visionaries and strategists

We have listened to the perceptions of those who live in the new urban areas, but now we enter into conversation with those who do not necessarily live in these areas but certainly are understood to have a substantial controlling influence upon them. In this chapter, therefore, our attention turns to questions of visions and strategy. Rather than gathering information from documents and policy papers, we hear some prominent people who are involved in formulating visions and working out or influencing strategies. We engage with nine eminent persons: three from the public sector or governmental establishments directly involved in, or guiding, regeneration in the Thames Gateway area; three from non-governmental organizations (NGOs) that work with, or advise, the public sector; and three from private companies that have a major stake in the regeneration projects in the area. The conversations are about vision and strategy in the Thames Gateway and all the conversation partners have some major involvement and stake in the Gateway project itself.

Conversation partners

From the public sector, we hear from two senior officials of the Thames Gateway establishment, one from the Thames Gateway itself and another from one of its regional partnerships, the Kent Thameside Delivery Board. We also hear from a Member of Parliament who has been involved in negotiations and discussions on the Gateway regeneration project and who represents a constituency within the Gateway area. These three conversation partners bring us more or less the official version of the Thames Gateway vision.

With regard to NGOs, two of our interviewees come from organizations that are funded and supported by the government but provide a more independent, and sometimes critical, perspective on the regeneration programme. One of them leads an umbrella body of social housing associations and groups which is responsible for managing affordable housing in some of the new developments. The other heads up an architectural group that advises local authorities on planning. We also hear from a senior official of a charity that advocates environmentally friendly regeneration. These three represent the organizations that do not have to defend government policies. They are able to raise critical questions about the regeneration process.

Our third category of interviewees represents the private or independent sector. Here we have the head of a private property development company which already is visibly involved in developing sites in the Gateway area. We listen to the senior official of a Church-related financial body which has put significant investment into a particular new urban area. We also hear from an architect of great reputation whose company has designed huge projects in this country and who raised concerns about the Thames Gateway project as it began to take shape.

After we listen to our conversation partners on various aspects of the Thames Gateway vision and strategy, we review some emerging concerns and questions. Although a general questionnaire was used as the framework for conversation, our partners did not focus equally on all questions, because their differing roles in the Gateway project meant that not every question was equally applicable to everyone. Some had a role in shaping the vision, whilst others inherited the vision as they came into their particular job. Some are actually responsible for the development that takes place; others are there simply to advise the strategists and planners. The questions we asked covered two broad areas: vision and strategy. We will therefore set out our questions under these two heads, and because the interviews were quite lengthy, we will endeavour to give a concise summary of the responses, using our interviewees' own words where possible.

Vision

The first set of questions centred upon vision: 'Where did the vision for the Thames Gateway region originate? To whom does the vision belong? How far have the local voices been heard? What are the key policies that shape the development? How has the vision been changed and modified and why? What was your role in the formation of the vision?'

The response of the Thames Gateway Official:

Thames Gateway is basically an economic project. It seeks to realize the economic potential of a part of the country that has not been as economically vibrant as other areas. People in this area are low-skilled and low-waged. We aim to achieve better employment opportunities, high-tech and commercial facilities. Second, there is also an environmental dimension to this vision: improving the quality of the surroundings in which people live. It is stewardship of creation. Brownfield stretches of land are to be turned into waterside sites. Third, it is a vision for an inclusive social context. It is development for all, for those who are already there and those who will be moving in. No one should feel left behind.

The vision for Thames Gateway may be traced as far back as Michael Heseltine's original vision for a south-east expansion down the River from the then new Docklands Development in London's old dockyards. John Prescott and Yvette Cooper and the Labour government then turned this into the vision as we have it now. It is the largest regeneration plan in West Europe. There are 1.5 million people already living in the Thames Gateway area; 300,000 new people are expected in this area by 2020. We are making provisions not really by creating new urban areas but mostly by strengthening the ones which are already there and by transforming brownfield sites into bright new places for work, living and leisure. Thames Gateway Strategic Partnership intends to provide 160,000 new homes between 2001 and 2016. The vision has not changed as such, but it has incorporated new possibilities because of the developments which were not there in the first place. Olympic opportunities are the best example for this. So the horizons of the vision enlarge. I share this vision fully and help its fulfilment by co-ordinating, guiding and planning various aspects of regeneration.

The Kent Thameside official:

It is not easy to trace the beginning of this vision for the regeneration of the Kent Thameside area. Part of the land, for example part of the Bluewater area, was originally agricultural. However, when tight controls over quarrying and landfill waste disposal were introduced, this restricted further acquisition of land for the quarrying companies. The available properties were quarried to the maximum, so companies had to rethink their strategy for their land. A large section of land just remained idle and rubbished. Blue Circle (later sold to Lafarge) began to make agreements with Land Securities for the development of certain sites. Companies then began to partner with Kent County Council in the early 1990s for planning developments in the unused land. The central government, faced with the demand for further housing, recognized the potential of the South-East area and realized that much was already going on there. Government's vision was one of consolidating all that was going on and all that was possible, with a commitment to affordable housing and environmental regeneration. Local voices have been heard through borough councils and Local Strategic Partnerships. The core transport elements of the vision for Kent Thameside – including the Ebbsfleet Valley, Channel Tunnel Rail Link and integrated transport – still remain at the heart of the vision and in that sense the vision has not changed. We have a public-transport-oriented approach. We trust that people will enjoy public transport and reduce private transport in the area.

The role of my organization, which is one of the sub-regional bodies within the Thames Gateway, is providing leadership for the development in the Kent Thameside area. We run certain projects directly, for example Employment Kent Thameside and the Green Grid (a plan for linking up the existing and new public green spaces in Kent Thameside by providing environment-friendly access routes between them). We also undertake studies and research on future development and currently we are doing this on flood risk, water and the housing market. Another role of the organization is co-ordinating funding applications: we have funded the Green Grid project, the Darenth Valley path and various consultancies. As there are so many players involved in this massive regeneration, conflicts of interests, misunderstandings and problems are natural. Therefore, we have the role of negotiating and problem-solving too.

The Member of Parliament:

Michael Heseltine's early dream of an 'East London corridor' recognized the potential of east of London for growth. John Prescott relaunched the idea because of the pressure for increased housing. It was basically about using brownfields, useless and contaminated land. Planning policy was changed to put brownfields first. I am not sure when the name Thames Gateway came into play. The vision and original concept came from the government. Yet local voices have been heard on matters of delivery. On the skills issue, there are several bodies working together. At community level, the voluntary sector and the faith communities are represented in the Delivery Board and in the local partnerships. SEEDA [the South-East England Development Agency] has commissioned a feasibility study to establish a Faith Observatory in partnership with Rochester Cathedral. Yet I accept that we haven't gone as far as we should have gone. Somehow people still do not feel that they are listened to. More dialogue is needed on building capacity and the environmental dimensions of regeneration.

The policies that shape the development are laid out in two documents: *The Sustainable Community Plan* (ODPM 2003) and *The Thames Gateway Interim Plan: Policy Framework* (DCLG 2006). Housing, economic growth, affordability, employment opportunity, environmental sustainability, inclusive community, skills and infrastructure/transport are the main emphases in these policy documents. But the vision for the Thames Gateway is one that constantly evolves. For example, new tourism possibilities for even mid-north Kent have come with Olympic hopes. This was unexpected and our current vision incorporates these aspirations and possibilities. But the core of the vision hasn't changed; the two basic elements, the best use of surplus land and demand for housing, are still the same. I have been personally involved at governmental level and as a member of the Regional Partnership that covers this area. This vision is very much my vision too.

We now move to our second group of interviewees – namely those from the non-governmental sector.

The housing group executive:

The Thames Gateway vision seems to belong to the government. The ordinary people living in the area proposed for development do not seem to be so enthusiastic about it; I don't get an impression that it is the people's vision. There is so much talk about 'sustainable communities', but the vision is not clear about how such communities can be established. The emphasis is clearly on housing units. But what would bind the people together as a community? Would a set of housing units and people living in those units naturally make up a community? We seem to force the formation of a community rather than letting communities emerge. Then there is the question about how we could fit in and care for the needs of those who cannot afford the highly priced housing units in a brand new housing complex or village. My group manages housing units for affordable housing serving a wide range of people, especially the poor and those with special needs. We manage most of the units earmarked as affordable and either rent them out or let tenants have shared ownership. We also discuss with the developers and planners about the specifications of new units when a new development is planned.

The policy for housing with an emphasis on high-density development is problematic in itself. The government wants more units and expects the investors to deliver quickly. But the game is in the court of private investors. Their vision is centred on quick returns. They rarely have a long-term commitment to the community. The vision has recently changed or developed, partly due to new factors like the London Olympics and partly due to the changing business interests of the investors. The units are getting smaller than we originally thought they would be. The justification for this is that the target group are young working-class people needing only small units. But what will happen when these families grow? The facilities in general as envisaged today would become inadequate for the future. It is a fact that not many community facilities are provided in the newly developed housing sites.

We note that since this interview the market has turned once again, one-bedroom apartments now saturating the market, so reducing returns for developers on this kind of planning.

The architectural adviser:

Regeneration as it happens today is a reality and it will continue to happen whether planned or unplanned. The vision of Thames Gateway is a sum total of all that is happening in the area. The government recognized the need for further housing and identified the Gateway area as the ideal location for planned development. My organization tries to think outside the box about the kind of development we need. We challenge the planners and architects with critical questions and helpful insights. The vision as it comes down to us from the establishment is still too vague to answer our questions adequately. One major question we are concerned about is the identity of the new community. If we excavate an ancient city we will come across some physical structures around which the community was organized. Religious and social institutions and establishments always played a major role. But the new plans do not have these as priorities. By building a physical structure now, we are deciding how a future community should be organized. With no centres to hold people together in community spirit, the new people will remain individuals or families unrelated to each other, yet living in the same locality and probably still attached to the distant original communities from where they came.

The voice of a community is often asked for. But at times these dialogues are without clear plan or purpose. Sometimes ordinary people are consulted on issues that even the experts are not clear about. Various options available are not explained to people. Some of these consultations do raise expectations that no one can ultimately meet. We as an organization try to a great extent to be in dialogue with local people in a meaningful way. We keep on engaging in discussions with planners, developers and local authorities, on the one hand asking them what exactly they are wanting, and on the other hand we talk with the community, asking them what they really want. We then seek to advise the major players in the game of regeneration on designs of development in the area.

The environmental charity executive:

The Thames Gateway vision has potential for delivering well for the people in the area, but there are aspects of the vision which need much clearer thinking and planning. One of the basic elements of this vision, namely brownfields, needs closer attention. The idea that brownfield sites – those where previous use is no longer desirable – are useless and uneconomic patches of land is not right in all cases. Many of the quarries, for example, were abandoned more than two decades ago and they have already developed in a natural way. Some of these areas could be nature conservation areas. A proper conservation assessment is required before condemning some brownfield sites as useless areas.

The overemphasis on the South-East as the growth area is not healthy and it is a major drawback in the government's vision for growth in terms of housing and commercial enterprise. The South-East is sinking due to geological causes. Flooding is a major issue to tackle and there has been no proper scientific analysis and long-term planning in the context of flood risk. There is talk about a new Thames Barrier, but there are consequences for that too which need to be taken into account. There are lots of unknowns in this process. On the other hand there is a significant scarcity of water in Kent and Essex in the dry season. To a great extent this scarcity could be met by recycling waste water. Even sewage water can be recycled and used for irrigation purposes. But all these ideas need long-term planning and decisions and there is no indication that they are being properly considered.

Having heard the view of those from the non-governmental sector, we move to our last group of visionaries and strategists – those from the private sector.

The chief executive of a private development company:

The vision of transforming neglected brownfield sites for the benefit of the people, both those who live in and around those areas and those who might want to move in there, originated from government, but it is now a vision shared by government, local authorities, landowners, developers and the people themselves. People would be happy to move to towns and cities if those places are made liveable. Government housing policy after the Second World War proved to be divisive as communities became divided and segregated with the coming of separated council housing estates. As responsible developers, we are trying to see that this kind of segregation does not take place in the new developments. In rural areas, both rich and poor people live side by side because they need each other. That is the kind of society we need to create in the Thames Gateway area. Chelmer in Chelmsford and Greenwich Village on the Thames are examples where our attempts to make sure that we have a truly mixed community have borne fruit. One cannot easily distinguish between those who are in fully owned, partly owned, or 'affordable' housing. They are all mixed and there is no separation between various sections of the community.

There are some weaknesses in the vision that comes down to us today from government and planners. This does not really think about the 'centres' that can bind the community together. For example, [Section] 106 agreements[1] do not take into account the fact that a place of worship can be a community facility that would be

---

[1] Section 106 of the Town and Country Planning Act 1990 allows a local planning authority to enter into a legally binding agreement or planning obligation with a land developer over a related issue, an obligation sometimes termed a 'Section 106 agreement'. Such agreements can act as major instruments for placing restrictions on developers, often requiring them to minimize the impact of their development on the local community, and to carry out tasks that will provide community benefits. For further information, see IDeA (2008).

central to community cohesion. Again, we easily forget that a sustainable community is one where people are able to live longer term, but if, because of short-term demand and pressure for fast delivery, developers go for mostly one-bedroom or two-bedroom flats, we are not making provision for a long-term future. People will have to leave the place and move to other areas as their families grow, and these new developments will then always remain as stopgap arrangements. You have to understand that the developers have to work with the limitations imposed by the existing market and therefore there has to be more dialogue on building sustainable communities between the government, local authorities, developers and the local people. The vision has not changed since its inception, but there is at least recently a better understanding of environmental issues and social and community needs than when we began.

The Church-body executive:

Regeneration is a socio-economic reality. It would happen whether the government planned it or not, but it is for the government to direct and guide the process with clearly laid out policies and laws. That is what the government is trying to do through its Thames Gateway initiative. In this case government has given a push for growth by earmarking a geographical area and identifying specific sites for development and pouring in considerable amounts of money to set up basic structures for coordinating and energizing regeneration in the Gateway area. But it is private investors who bring in the real money and take the work forward. We have claimed a stake in this process by investing substantial funds for a particular project, buying 1,500 acres of land and planning residential units, business space and community facilities there. We get the planning permission and then allot the work to developers. It will be a brand new village with all the essential facilities for the inhabitants. Our intention is to maximize returns, but we do it in the best way possible by offering people a first-class environment to live in. The policies that we use to guide regeneration are related to housing, sustainable community, education, transport and environment. Provision for educational and health facilities are provided within the proposed development. Our vision hasn't changed but the details of plans have undergone a lot of changes as a result of dialogue with local people and consultation with authorities and others involved in the process. We have had two one-day seminars with local people about the needs and the design. People understand what we are doing and we feel they now share our vision.

The independent architect:

This largest regeneration area in Europe has never had any overall plan or vision. The Thames Gateway idea goes back to the Tory government two decades ago. Since then, armies of consultants have been engaged to study how we might deliver 200,000 homes and the infrastructure that the current Labour government says is required here. These housing targets could actually be met largely within East London, near existing infrastructure, with only a small requirement to grow in the towns of North Kent and South Essex. There is in fact room enough for another two central Londons in the East of London between Canary Wharf and the Dartford Crossing. To save the community and the environment, London's employees ought to be accommodated within London and the future of the outer areas beyond would be better ensured both socially and economically with a green-based vision quite separate from the housing-shortage numbers game that the government plays.

The central issue is one of long-term, urban and rural environmental quality and this has not found a place in the grand 'vision'. No one has clearly presented or even conceived of such a thing. If you ask for an overall plan for the Thames Gateway, you will get either wordy generalizations that could apply to anywhere in Britain, or smaller-scale local, detailed and insular initiatives or projects that were independently under way before the Thames Gateway was declared. There are no clear indications in any of the published documents about making the project a showcase for environmental industry and innovation in new agricultural methods, alternative forms of power generation, waste management and energy conservation. A creative, physical, overarching plan for flood control is also missing. Overall, what we have now in the name of the Thames Gateway is just 'rebranding' that which we already had and there is no indication about changing direction or facing the real concerns that need addressing.

Strategy

The second major strand in our interviews centred upon the question of strategy: 'If you did not have to follow the "rules", would you do it differently? What are the constraints on Utopia? How will the development affect existing communities? Would you want to live in the place which you have built?'

The Thames Gateway official:

I would be personally more happy if the whole Thames Gateway were operated as one strategic area, with the same people involved in the work of the whole area rather than having several areas with too many different groups or teams of people driving the process. Another concern is money. It would be helpful to know how much money is going to be available in the next five years or ten years, so that we could plan accordingly. Another constraint is at governmental level. Different departments of the government should have to work together to create quality living places. I wish there were some mechanism to get the departments to think in a coordinated manner. I would like to see everyone in the Thames Gateway area knowing about what is happening and feeling proud of it. I am in fact proud of the overall vision of the Gateway, not just as someone having a leading role in the project, but as a resident within the area, and I will continue to live in the area.

The Kent Thameside official:

There is less public or governmental control over the kind of development taking place than you might think. In the housing developments that have already been completed in the North Kent area, the proportion of affordable units is much lower than that recommended by government. In certain areas it is mostly the big investors who have bought houses *en bloc* and therefore the house prices are much higher than for similar properties in the locality. First-time buyers are pushed out of the market. This is a strategic failure. One of the big constraints is the conflicting interests of the parties involved: government, landowners, developers, financiers and the local residents. Developers build housing units with a motif of quick and maximum returns. With no public control over the process, the newly built residential complexes could look socially uninspiring even if they were visually attractive. Some of the developers could end up creating dormitory communities. I try my best to argue for, and pursue the cause of, socially attractive and inclusive developments that would enhance life for both the existing communities and the new residents.

The Member of Parliament:

If you are talking about strategy, I would like to see things done slightly differently. First, I would like to see that a network is set up to get the message of Thames Gateway across to the people and develop the local community's understanding of the potential and possibilities of this project. Second, I would deal with one of the constraints on the Thames Gateway vision: the increasing number of organizations dealing with the Thames Gateway. There are too many of them and the number has to come down. Each of them seems to work independently with its own agenda and goals. True partnership is not yet achieved. Utopia expects people to be working together for a common purpose, but this is certainly not always the practice. But in spite of all these limitations and constraints communities are benefited. The existing communities also benefit from the new job opportunities that are being created in the area because the commercial initiatives and financial investment in the area contribute to local growth. I would surely, and I do, live in the place I help build.

The housing group executive:

I would like to stick to the plans rather than constantly see them changing. Changes must be accepted for valid reasons only. For example, a 106 agreement is designed to assist in funding community facilities. But in the Isle of Sheppey it funded the construction of a road! This was money meant for some community facility. The lack of resources is really a problem. Private developers are pushed to build the maximum number of housing units. Under such pressure, developers go for smaller units in order just to meet the short-term needs. This short-termism is seen in both planning and resourcing issues. There is some lack of vision on the side of policy-makers too. The future is not really envisaged; the community facilities that are planned in most of the developments prove to be only just enough to meet the demands of the community as it is today. No one seems to ask questions about the needs of the communities into the future. Lack of infrastructure is another constraint. There is no emphasis on developing the necessary infrastructure alongside, and at the same time as, the housing. Among the effects of this on the community is the chance of segregation. We seem to end up with new developments with all the facilities on one hand, and the existing communities which, after being disrupted by the adjacent new build, are left unsupported and unprovided for. There is also lack of self-criticism. We still haven't learnt the lessons from our experience of building housing complexes in the post-war scenario.

The architectural adviser:

We are a body meant to think outside the box and in that sense critically of some of the rules and strategies. Yes, we would like to do things differently. There is, for example, a question of identity for the new communities. We would like to see community centres – both social and religious – in each new village that would provide structures for development of the new communities. We would also like to address the danger of unbalancing existing communities. It seems if we do very well in the 'development' process, the middle class and the well-to-do people will move in; if we do very badly, the new sites will end up as ghettos. Careful thinking and planning are required about the nature of the development we should go for and I think that that strategic analysis is usually missing. As we are not living in a utopia, all the constraints of the real world are there for us to face. Lack of finance and infrastructure are important. There is also short-termism to put up with. Government wants the quick delivery of housing units, investors want a quick and maximum return on their money, developers want to construct the kind of houses that would be in demand for the short term. There is no long-term strategy or vision for the future. Only the public sector can really undertake this long-term planning. The private sector does not have a long-term concern but it is that sector which drives the current plans and vision.

The environmental charity executive:

We like to see a vision that includes improving the area for people who are already there, although it cannot be exclusively for them. In the rhetoric, this is usually part of the vision, but the strategies do not support that aspect of the vision. I wonder whether the Thames Gateway project will turn out to be something like the development at Docklands, where locals were pushed out. Local people should be equipped with particular skills if they are to benefit from new employment opportunities, but there is no strategy for this. On the transport side, on one hand we talk about enticing people to use public transport, but on the other we widen the motorways, attracting more drivers. The shortage of money in public funds is a real constraint. This leads to dependence on private money and so less commitment to the wider society. The Thames Gateway project can work only if different players with different roles work together and complement each other. No one player can achieve its target without the others. For example, the central government is concerned about housing, employment and the economy. Local authorities are concerned to look after infrastructure and community facilities, including education and transport. The developers have to deliver services in such a way that their profit is assured. Inevitably there are conflicts between these different players in the game. People in general are now showing increasing concern about the environmental implications of this massive regeneration – air and water pollution, loss of public open spaces, flood risk and so on – but there is no strategy to alleviate these fears and take remedial measures.

The chief executive of a private development body:

A major constraint on strategy is the lack of understanding about the vision among the local authorities and existing communities. They seem to have fears about our projects. They need therefore to know how the project is going to benefit them. Lack of money is another obvious constraint. We could do with more money but already the regeneration and new projects are helping the existing communities by enhancing their life. The whole area as a consequence will be witnessing tremendous economic growth, the benefits of which will be shared by the existing communities as well as the new communities. We have already completed some projects with a substantial number of housing units and they are built with the purpose of promoting an inclusive community. I would be happy to live in one of those places myself.

The Church-body executive:

I wish the process were a lot quicker. We would have already developed some sites by this time. Planning and designing a project takes an unduly long time because we have to deal with various parts or departments of the local authority separately. So we would wish that the rules were different. Utopia is not the same for everyone. Landowners and the developers like to take money out at the earliest opportunity. Occupiers want a world of facilities and quality. Some local people do not want any development at all! The planning system brings people's concerns to the table and uses its controlling and regulatory powers to steer the process forward. The existing communities stand to gain from these major developments in and around their areas. Added community facilities and improved and increased transport are definitely going to help them. I would live in a place I have helped to build.

The independent architect:

> The point is that there isn't any comprehensive strategy for Thames
> Gateway. Neither are there enough rules to control and guide this
> kind of unnecessary expansion. These two factors are the main con-
> straints on Utopia. There is no strategy to enhance the area's valu-
> able and fragile eco-systems. A new kind of National Park would be
> the best way to confront major sustainability issues faced by the
> region, but unfortunately we have instead the expansion of urban
> into rural areas without using up the available unused land within
> London. There are no concrete plans in the area to handle the waste
> which will be generated in the area, which could be converted into
> energy and useful by-products. Our non-planning incompetence is
> leading us to a town-planning free-for-all. This growth is going to
> be environmentally disastrous, so both the existing and the new
> communities will find life less comfortable than it is now.

Emerging concerns and questions

These responses raise important concerns. Those who represent the
government and those who undertake the development complain
about the slowness of the whole process, while those who look at
the process either from an environmental or a community-oriented
perspective feel that the process is going ahead without a proper
consideration of the dangers involved.

A primary question that arises from our interview conversations
is about the 'how' of community-building. Does a community
emerge slowly of itself, or can we just create a community by implementing our plans and strategies? Even if we accept the argument
that we are only providing the basic facilities and structure for a
community to emerge of itself, the question remains whether we
are leaving space and opportunity for the necessary future development and changes to take place organically. The plans that have
been made available to us of different sites within the Thames
Gateway seem to assume that the planners know what the communities will need and that developers can provide those basic facilities
before the communities arrive on the scene. Every portion of the
land is already allocated for some purpose. In a natural situation,
as the community grows it should be able to recognize its own
needs and make provision for those needs. But the people who

will inhabit the brand-new areas will not be left with the freedom to develop the infrastructure and facilities as and when the needs arise.

If the community itself is not going to have much hold on its own future, who else will have control? As we repeatedly heard, it is private money that creates growth today. It is largely down to the private investors and developers to decide the details of the projects. For example, when the size of the housing units is decided by the developers, determined by what is marketable, there is no reason to think that this will prove to be the need of the emerging community in the future. Smaller units will sell more quickly in one market but in time this could lead to either a dormitory community or a floating community. People will live in these units for a shorter time, either until their families grow or until they have had the chance to buy a bigger unit. This is not an example of a 'sustainable community'. In effect, it is the private investors and developers, acquiescing to the dictates of a short-term market, who decide what kind of development we are going to get, and this will constrain what sort of community we can build – if 'community' is possible at all. There are signs here of a neo-feudal arrangement of ownership and management of the land, where ordinary people do not enjoy the freedom to shape their own lives and any control over the resources that shape their economy is in the hands of their masters.

What is also lost in this process is concern for the environment and the well-being of existing communities. In the mad rush for faster development, vital questions about environment are neglected. Energy and water conservation, waste management, flood-risk control and the quality of construction are certainly part of the current rhetoric, but there is little sign of careful and detailed research and dialogue. Neither is there any overall strategy or detailed plan to address these concerns.

Existing communities do put up with a lot of disruption from the whole process. But what do they receive by way of compensation? Fastrack is a test case. Fastrack is a rapid bus service with dedicated road lanes in the Kent Thameside. When it was proposed there was an excited expectation that it would connect the old and new communities with a faster transport system. But one major factor in deciding the route has been the availability of money from investing developers. Developers are happy to invest money for a road going through their own new developments because that will push up the price of their properties. But it turns out that the existing communities in Northfleet will not have the service of Fastrack in future (even though it does currently run through Northfleet). We cannot expect private developers to be interested in the welfare of the existing communities, which may be in competition with their new developments. There is also fear about the future of existing high streets and town centres as the major economic activity gravitates towards the commercial and business areas in the new developments, with their purpose-built shopping centres and new infrastructures. There is also a legitimate concern that the residential units in the new development sites will benefit only those who have salaries large enough to avail themselves of the expensive new facilities and fashionable amenities. As the ordinary local people are economically powerless to join this club, a new community of well-salaried people emerges at the expense of overall community cohesion.

According to most of our interviewees, there is a lack of long-term planning and vision in the current proposals and plans for the Thames Gateway. Central government, local authorities and the private players involved are working with short-term goals, lacking both overall vision and integrated strategy. When the initial plans for the development in the Ebbsfleet Valley were released, these included four primary schools within Gravesham Borough. Now, as the plans have reached the final stage, only one primary school remains, the opinion being that the new community may not have enough children for four schools. One primary school for a population equal to that of the city of Chichester is a bit strange! The short-termism guiding current development indicates our failure to project a sustainable community into the future – perhaps young people do not have children of school age now, but some time surely they will?

As the government has repeatedly admitted, what is lacking is joined-up thinking. The different departments responsible for essential services – for example, education, health and transport – are not thinking together. They need to look at their investment in the area on the basis of the human development envisaged in the area, not on the basis of current and short-term market demand. Before the onslaught of neo-liberalism it was the government who funded newly developed communities, rather than leaving the whole process to private investors and developers. Ultimately someone has to be responsible overall, and that responsibility surely should be in the hands of a democratically accountable government.

That leads us to the nature of the vision itself. Where do we find the right vision for a development like the Thames Gateway? Whose vision should it be? If the people of the Thames Gateway do not share the enthusiasm shown by the major players in the game, especially the private investors and developers, how can the process bring about sustainable communities across the Thames Gateway area? Why is it that the government is still failing to convince the existing communities that these projects are good for them? Part of the problem is that the consultations with the existing communities, which we consider necessary, have not been taken seriously. The local community's opinions have not been taken fully into account while revising the plans. This is why there has been no serious attempt, for example, to address the environmental concerns involved. As we have observed above, the changes in the Fastrack route are primarily at the insistence of the developers, not in accord-ance with the evident needs of the existing communities.

People are not enthusiastic. Environmental agencies and experts have reservations. Even many of the much-proclaimed purposes of the housing projects are not achieved. For example, the cheapest 'affordable' housing unit in a recently built Kent Thameside project costs £170,000, a much higher price than that of an existing unit of comparable size in the same locality. The government promises affordable housing for a price around £60,000, but surely it is simply ridiculous of the government to expect private builders to act as agents of welfare: that is not their task. Above all, it is hard to see how sustainable communities can be established in a ready-made and, to some extent, artificial context when so much is based on a market economy. Is there an alternative vision or plan, or is it largely an exercise in rhetoric?

References

DCLG (Department of Communities and Local Government), *Thames Gateway Interim Plan: Policy Framework*. Communities and Local Government Publications, Wetherby, 2006.

IDeA (Improvement and Development Agency for Local Government), 'Section 106 Agreement', <www.idea.gov.uk/idk/core/page.do?pageid=71631> (accessed 20 June 2008).

ODPM (Office of the Deputy Prime Minister), *Sustainable Communities: Building for the Future*. Office of the Deputy Prime Minister, Wetherby, 2003. The Plans for each Region were published in the same year at <www.communities.gov.uk/publications/communities/sustainablecom­munitiesbuilding>.

5

The impact on the public sector

'I can't keep up with it all' is a phrase that most people will hear repeatedly, whether it is the new technology, the latest health advice, our workplace demands or our home lives; in every area of life there is incessant change and incessant pressure on people to do more, have more, make more or be more. The pressure-cooker environment of 'Utopia creation' which usually accompanies urban regeneration, growth and change is something felt not only by local communities as they live through this time of transformation, but also by many who work with these communities and their residents. For those in the public sector there is a huge new remit to fulfil amidst an ever-shifting landscape of physical change and political and bureaucratic reorganization.

This chapter explores the experiences of some of those who are working in the public sector at this time in our history of massive urban regeneration initiatives. Our interviews took place with workers employed by a local police force, a board of education, a further education college, a primary care trust, a local education authority and a London community work department. It immediately became clear that what were once clear boundaries and defined patterns of work have changed. Workers are feeling disorientated or having to carve out new ways of functioning effectively. New government directives and measures challenge previously understood working methods. Short-term contracts and job losses add to all this pressure as public servants try to engage with communities who are, during this time of regeneration and development, vulnerable, disenfranchised, chaotic and unsure of their future. In 2000 the government's Department of Environment, Transport and the Regions commissioned a report, *Living in Urban England* (Todorovic and Wellington 2000) and two of the key findings are worth noting here. First, people living in urban areas are much more likely to be dissatisfied than those in suburban and rural areas (and there is also a correlation between this dissatisfaction and urban deprivation). Second, people living in London and other metropolitan areas are more likely to think that their area has changed over the past two years. Of those people that identified the change, twice as many thought it has been negative rather than positive. The report says that this was particularly evident amongst residents living in the social rented sector: they generally felt far more pessimistic about their future and they also believed that the schools and job opportunities associated with their neighbourhood were getting worse. Additionally they identified crime and personal safety as being negative features of urban areas. This is the urban context in which public-sector workers are delivering services. We interviewed a wide variety of such workers, including a commissioner and director (of public services) together with some of the grassroots workers they were managing, as well as others working with the police service, primary education, adult education, community work, and health.

The search for Utopia begins?

The current New Labour government has aimed to modernize Britain quite radically and has tried to attack the causes and consequences of poverty, crime, poor health and low educational attainment. New Labour has made considerable attempts within government to have a 'joined-up' approach to working for the objectives designed to address these societal problems. To this end there have been government reforms and new units set up, such as the Social Exclusion Unit and the health action zones (HAZs). The government launched the health action zone initiative in 1997. Twenty-six HAZs were set up as seven-year pilot projects 'to explore mechanisms for breaking through current organisational boundaries to tackle inequalities and deliver better services' (NICE 2008). HAZs were meant not only to improve health outcomes and reduce health inequalities, but also to act as 'trailblazers' for new ways of local working. HAZs have now been incorporated into the development of primary care trusts. Indices of multiple deprivation (IMD) have been calculated and the ideas of capacity-building and social cohesion have been made key aims in the plans for regeneration schemes and new urban developments. The private sector has been investing in this new regeneration industry alongside the government, so all sectors have experienced the challenging world of working in partnership. This new system of working in partnership with a joined-up approach and joined-up policies is an effort to ensure that the service user will receive a package that saves trudging from one service to another, but is also based upon the best use of meagre resources. Does this raise the confidence of the community in the public services that are being delivered?

The experience of working in partnership

Our interviewees told us that for them, what working in partnership amounted to was the introduction of an 'input/output'-driven mechanism where everything received by each service user was logged and monitored in some format or another. However, the increased paperwork and failures in communication, especially at local government level, have reflected badly on local public-service delivery, especially for those who have complex and deep-seated problems and are socially excluded. Yet whilst individuals in new communities need coherent and relevant services which they have the opportunity to influence, they find themselves waiting upon the distant development of huge strategy documents and complex policies which bear little relation to local experience and the public services they need to receive.

The qualities we most value in society seem to be breaking down: we appear to see a growing lack of trust, disrespect, relationship breakdown, power struggles, lack of compassion and injustice, and this is mirrored in the organizations we have investigated. Breakdowns of understanding across not only the public sector but also across inter-sector structures are a challenge we will recognize in the stories of the public-sector workers included in our research. The language barriers, institutional complexities and organizational acronyms are difficult to work with, whilst the great variety of funding strategies, implementation plans, working methodologies and value systems creates both a demanding and stimulating new culture in which to try to function as a carer. These challenges and opportunities are heightened when working within newly built regeneration areas.

In the new urban areas the ethos of partnership has an important impact upon service provision. Whilst workers can appreciate the importance of holistic care, the reality of competition between the development and building partners is mirrored in the competitive ethos of government departments. Values of different organizations vary considerably, agendas can clash, the understanding of each other's agency can be poor, and competitive power struggles can arise that inhibit the way partners work. Working in partnership also tends to favour the bigger players, the smaller groups being less likely to be invited to the table. There can be suspicion about sharing information and resources when providers of services are made to bid against one another. This is especially the case when the voluntary third sector engages in the partnership. So performance management structures hinder rather than encourage a culture of collaboration and cooperation.

The areas within the Thames Gateway churn out a great deal of flowing rhetoric about how new and inclusive public-sector programmes are making qualitative differences in new urban areas, but lack of delivery creates a loss of faith in provision on the part of both worker and client. However, we discerned a remarkable degree of enthusiasm and energy amongst the public-sector workers to do their best for the local communities and the people they serve, and this is hopeful and encouraging.

Holistic versus target-driven approaches in public-service provision

In their Demos report, David Wilkinson and Elaine Appelbee (1999) suggest the public sector needs to get back in touch with the public, and those we interviewed fully endorsed that suggestion. Users must be allowed to influence how and why services are delivered. This is crucial if society is to flourish with active citizens who have broken free from the chains of marginalization, humiliation and exclusion. However, the workers we interviewed for this chapter were unable to offer appropriate services due to pressure on time and resources. They struggle to close the gap between demand and adequate delivery, yearning to reach the people who are most in need.

Since London is a global economic leader undergoing rapid change and development, we would have hoped to observe investment in service provision, with workers having the resources needed for empowering local people to shape the services they receive.

When asked, 'What are your perceptions of what is happening in new urban developments at the moment where there is change and regeneration taking place?', the public-sector workers we interviewed were negative and offered painful reactions as they struggled with well-intentioned public services that were unable to deliver.

There was an overwhelming feeling that regeneration is a top-down and government-led process, driven more by economics than anything else. What our public-sector interviewees notice is that regeneration is good for those who are well off, who have access to choice and are able to purchase what they want to fulfil their lives. The wealthy can shop in one place, live in another and socialize in yet another. For such people there seems no need for a local neighbourhood as such because they can purchase or 'pick 'n mix' their lifestyle and communities according to current desires or trends, even down to the details of what shopping they want and the time slot they choose to have it delivered. For the poor, however, financial choices do not exist. One respondent believed that 'The class structure still exists in Britain and it is overlooked in the work of the public sector.'

Public space and personal choice

Living in a regenerated area can bestow a new status, particularly if you are in a river-frontage warehouse conversion or a centrally located hub. Anywhere along the Thames with new housing or business developments, wealthy, often short-term residents are moving in who can afford a lifestyle which allows them to opt out of the local community if they choose to. Public services to these new communities can be limited because some residents opt out and 'purchase' school, gym, private health care and concièrge security services. In other words, these groups can choose to 'secede' from locally accountable and democratically elected public bodies, thus replacing a public domain with a private one.

However, the public workers we interviewed recognized that, for those who are poor, choice is taken away, homes and surrounding landscapes are changed without their knowledge, and they are forced to comply with often unwelcome regeneration strategies and initiatives. Land that was once the local domain of working people in trades such as ship-building or dock work, and was therefore part of the psyche and deep-rooted history of local communities, is ripped up, blocked up and built on, and made inaccessible to them. In some areas in South London the local estate people are no longer able to access the riverside paths, because new gated apartment blocks have been built on the river frontage. Only a long and arduous campaign by an elderly people's group has ensured that a small gate is left open during the day to allow access for local residents to the river. This demonstrates how extremely hard it is for local residents to be heard and how their vital intelligence about how their area ticks is so often ignored. What passes for consultation is an insult to their thorough knowledge of their area. They may be moved out of their homes, even when other dependent family members are residing nearby, and decanted temporarily into new dwellings, with the insecurity of not knowing whether they will be moved back to the place they know. In an era when family breakdown is at its highest, this is not a helpful way of supporting people! Regeneration can be preceded by fragmentation. This fragmentation is then a living, working reality for public-sector deliverers who are trying to re-establish a community and a network of services to support the people who have been torn apart during the redevelopment phase.

The Joseph Rowntree Foundation report, *Effective Participation in Anti-Poverty and Regeneration Work and Research* (Beresford and Hoban 2005), found that powerlessness is central to people's experience of poverty and disadvantage. Conventional bureaucratic and managerial 'top-down' approaches to participation have little success. People are much more likely to get involved in community consultation and programmes if they have a strong sense that something tangible and worthwhile is going to come out of it. For example, the Joseph Rowntree report says, 'People living in poverty have been taught to believe their opinions don't count; they may need to go through a long process before feeling confident in articulating their views.' Further, it highlights the significant issue of structural constraints, noting that 'while agencies often want one "community perspective" many different perspectives may exist, some more acceptable than others'.

The Joseph Rowntree research reinforces the fact that there are many bridges to build between those trying to deliver services in new and existing urban communities and those receiving these services. Large numbers of people on urban estates have few personal choices, and so public services are essential to their lives. Living in a vast new urban zone with next to no local amenities, little public transport, and an ethos of competitive individualism serves to isolate and disempower those who are already struggling. The Joseph Rowntree report uncovered the disjointed way that local services are delivered and the way this exacerbates the gap between the haves and have-nots, which in turn can lead to tensions across communities where wealthier areas have access to a variety of services and poorer areas do not.

In new urban areas such as Thames Gateway the transience of individuals is a huge issue. Tenants in the process of being decanted, asylum-seekers, those looking for work and those who work on short-term contracts all move around at very short notice. Where once it was easy to locate families or individuals needing services, or consistent education, there is no longer an assurance that residents will be established and rooted. New housing developments also result in significant increases in population and this puts services under more strain. The increasing proportion of residents belonging to minority ethnic groups produces a wonderful and diverse mix, but these groups require a great diversity of services. However, before one can even get to the point of delivery there are language and cultural barriers to cross. For example, in Southwark Borough alone 117 different languages are known to be spoken. If public services are to be provided to new citizens such as these, we must radically rethink how services are commissioned, managed and influenced if we are to avoid fundamental failures. When people fall through the net of service delivery and basic care provision because of such difficulties of access, it is a shameful indictment of the service sector and our society. Some respondents said that their priority in care provision had in fact now become focused on ease of access.

Complex needs in new urban areas

Our interviewees reported that in the newly developed urban areas there has been an increase in need and its complexity, especially among the poorest. For example, one interviewee from Hackney, right on the edge of the Thames Gateway, estimates that in the last two years there has been a 10 per cent increase in admissions of Bangladeshis to their psychiatric wards. Some argue that this is attributable to persecution and discrimination, often based on race and class, exacerbated by the lack of public spaces to meet across the cultures and a dearth in the provision of translators and people to support and make possible positive interactions between different community groups and members. Loss of investment in these front-line, yet simple, initiatives and resources results in personal pain for some, greater disintegration of the community, and eventually a greater cost to public services.

The recent deaths of knife-crime victims from urban regeneration areas has highlighted a form of unrest in local communities that is complex and indicates a society that has, perhaps, failed to listen to its marginalized groups and sought instead an individualized and atomistic, competitive culture. According to our interviewees from the Metropolitan Police, the crime scene has been changing – whilst some areas of criminal activity have decreased there has been more domestic violence, gang warfare, knife crime and human trafficking.

One respondent, when asked about their perception of the current regeneration in their community, replied, 'What community? We live side by side – we work side by side, but there is no interrelationship.' This might help to explain why gangs of youths in our localities are now so powerful. In some ways they are creating their own communities. These gangs might be examples of negative social capital but they appear to function as communities none the less, with internal structures, hierarchies, allies, visions and missions. More often than not their theme is respect, be it for territory, people or ideals.

Problems creating social capital in new urban areas

In his book *Bowling Alone: The Collapse and Revival of American Community*, Robert Putnam utilizes the concept of social capital, with 'bonding' referring to the strong social network established wihin homogeneous groups of people between their members (Putnam 2000). According to Putnam and his followers, social capital is a key component of building and maintaining democracy, but it is declining in the United States, where there is little trust in government and lower levels of civic participation. This thesis appears now to apply to the United Kingdom, and its effects are being felt by those who deliver public services and who see those in need becoming increasingly isolated from their local communities, especially in the newly built urban areas, where there is no built-in community but many pressures to isolate individuals and households from one another. Despite the challenges, many people working in the public sector in the midst of this vast ocean of change are hugely dedicated, highly motivated and driven to care for those to whom they strive to provide public services. They struggle to find effective ways of working so that those whose lives are affected by the ever-changing urban environment might be enabled to fulfil their potential, achieve what they want to achieve in their lives, and receive the care and support they need.

Against this background the evidence from our research suggests that widespread disillusionment is still arising from the new urban developments. Some respondents said that within the communities in which they work, many residents are feeling unsettled, fearful and stressed by the amount of change taking place around them. These stressful elements include fear of the unknown and uncertainty as to what will happen to the area they know, how it will affect their lives, and what sort of people will be coming into the regenerated or newly built area. The pulling down of buildings, the disruption of transport, the changing landscape of glass and steel skyscrapers, flashy apartments and estates with minimal social housing are encroaching upon the meagre space they still inhabit. People are feeling lost and overwhelmed amidst the regeneration schemes all around them. They cannot keep up with the changes and for some this leads to anger, for others isolation and for others a sense of being swallowed up by the business of regeneration and therefore not being able to do anything about it.

These are huge issues for those in the public services. Our question to them was therefore: 'What is it like trying to deliver a public service in these circumstances?' As might be expected, this question provoked a wide variety of responses, but there was a common feeling that the work was still both challenging and rewarding. One of the major challenges arose from the demands of the governmental structures on the service providers due to the competitive, and therefore potentially mistrustful, regeneration culture within which they now found themselves – for example, job-sharing, short-term contracts and bureaucratic paperwork systems which change frequently and are highly time-consuming, complicate the work. The continually changing targets and the differing ways of measuring outputs and outcomes are draining the confidence of public-sector workers, heightening their stress, and contributing to the decline of morale in the sector. Pressure on individual workers has gone up and job satisfaction has gone down, as they spend more and more hours on paperwork rather than working with the people they want to serve. Whilst the regeneration consultants tend to turn up in their expensive cars, the low salaries for public-service providers are unattractive and recruitment therefore targets young and inexperienced applicants. Whilst it is important to employ young people and train tomorrow's experts, there is also a need for experienced workers to offer their skills and knowledge to the service. It is disconcerting to note the number of staff sickness days taken and the huge numbers of people who can't wait to retire. One respondent said, 'Thatcher's '80s government got rid of the fat, Major's '90s got rid of the flesh and New Labour are attacking the bones.' This comment reflects the feeling that the sector is on its knees, with some of its buildings being shut down or even converted into housing units by the regeneration industry. An interviewee commented, 'Our sector is currently surviving on the commitment of its workers.'

Linked to this increasing sense of low morale are the perceptions from many public-sector workers that the training and skills they received when starting work are far removed from the requirements of the job they do in today's world. A lot of training nowadays is done by outside training consultancies at huge cost to the sector.

Internal training teams have been disbanded and either made redundant or redirected to different posts, reinforcing the sense that little importance is attached to staff learning, thereby further reducing workers' sense of worth.

Hopeful signs for public-service delivery in new urban areas

Nevertheless, all is not gloom! One respondent said that the pressure in the sector at the moment can be very exciting too: 'Crisis can bring out the best in people. There are actions that need to be taken and there is a force upon the teams to deliver the very best way they can to their group of users, despite the obstacles that may be in their way.' For some, the crises which the new urban areas are experiencing are forcing them to adapt a 'can-do' attitude that works hard to ensure that people on the receiving end do not struggle unnecessarily.

Despite this, the weight of a bureaucratic and conservative ethos in management impedes the coalface workers in the new urban areas, who are more aware of the novelty of the challenge than are the office mandarins. One respondent said, 'Any sense of trying to explore new ways of working can be quickly squashed for the sake of working in a way that has been established for a long time. Therefore, the opportunities of offering a reflexive service [a service from which both worker and client benefit reciprocally] in these new circumstances are limited. It is easier to go through the prescribed procedures than to challenge a policy or system which has been dictated from on high.' One interviewee said that one of the most frustrating things about the job was 'working for an institution that preferred the comfort of the mainstream to working creatively or with the marginalized and excluded'. Another said, 'Unless there is an investment in time and patient understanding from the sector to work with local people who receive their services, then these services will be stifled by their current systems.' Strategic planning for the new urban areas is not easy given the present ways of operating, especially where some public services adopt a ten-year strategy but have only committed a budget for a three-year period. This makes it very difficult to offer services to new communities, where the needs are as yet unknown, and it seems ridiculous to assume that people's needs or statutory provision requirements will not develop over a ten-year period. Some managers optimistically rate their ability to predict the size of populations moving into new urban areas, but as to who these populations will turn out to be, where they might come from and what needs they might bring with them, surely is difficult to predict.

Such worries are reinforced further when respondents report that they do not have quality monitoring systems but have to work with rigid spreadsheets that insist on putting people into predesigned boxes. A system which allocates needs to the people on the receiving end is not helpful. New urban developments attract a wide range of people with diverse needs. 'This is a time to explore new ways of working by using the intelligence that these new communities bring with them,' said one informant. 'Britain has never seen change like this before; therefore we cannot rely on systems that have always worked before. There needs to be in place a mechanism which allows for service delivery to be friendlier and more effective for those on the receiving end.' Some primary care trusts, the local embodiment of the National Health Service, have tried to get closer to their patients by arranging patient forums and cultivating a wide variety of partners within the health action zones who discuss and devise service provision. But the reality is that these are usually un-representative groups of people – the able and the articulate. Other voices are not heard and therefore provision is not appropriately constructed.

'The influence of politics in the sector can be frustrating,' said another worker. 'After each election, new directives are issued asking the sector to change something or do more of something else.' The shifting sand of public policy demands on which many public-sector workers are asked to work is a further destabilizing factor in a sector that already feels demoralized. Despite all these challenges and disappointments, one worker voiced the view of many when she said, 'most staff, including managers, are still decent people who have a strong empathy for the communities they work with and they will put themselves out to make a difference to the lives of those people.' This was a positive response which emphasized that, though public-sector workers struggle in many areas, for a good number the beneficial effects they produce on the ground is still what drives them to put up with what happens in the office. The work done at the local level or on a one-to-one basis is what motivates the workers and is a credit to the service. One interviewee said that 'the work being done in homes with minority groups is teaching us about [the] cultural capabilities that should be built into any of our services.' This kind of learning is different from what can be taught on a course, for it is comes from hands-on experience over a period of time and provides realistic intelligence for challenging established modes of working. Management teams who are keen to listen to their ground-force workers are a crucial factor here, because these teams are then able to weave together the reality of delivery with the desires of government and the strategic and financial directions within the organization or sector. This indeed was the government's wish when John Prescott, then Deputy Prime Minister, wrote in a major policy paper, 'There is no one-size-fits-all solution. Our policies are based on engaging local people in partnership for change designed to meet their needs' (DETR 2000: 3). As one of our respondents told us, 'Having a local and face-to-face approach has produced the most significant of changes in my local area. Systematically working across the area has been a brilliant way of working – it has built up trust and people have enjoyed seeing a "face" to this public service.' A similarly positive comment emerged from a worker who now has a job in a local borough with the opportunity of getting out of the organization's office to be amongst the new urban communities, finding out about the residents, their lives, their interests, their faith, their connections, etc. All this knowledge helps the borough and public-service providers find relevant ways of working with these newly arrived groups: 'This aspect of the work is so much more rewarding than having to sit in the office typing up the paperwork!' This resonated with another respondent, who was working in an area of massive change and large regeneration initiatives. Where, in order to engage with local people, expensive lunches were provided to encourage their attendance and participation in the consultation processes, but she now found that simply going out to people, meeting with them in their own local places and talking with them one to one, had a much greater impact on service delivery. She found herself able to get the information she needed and to work more closely with service users, to the increased satisfaction of all concerned. This is a reversion to old, well-tried methods of putting local people before all else, listening carefully and forming provision accordingly, rather than allowing the over-whelming impact of the new urban areas to determine a more bureaucratically controlled and top-down approach. And these old methods seem to be paying off.

Conclusion

Providing resources will always be a challenge and the public policy world we now live in is a testament to good intentions but wasted resources. When public-sector personnel work collaboratively and holistically alongside the local people, this promotes human flourishing far more effectively than anything else, even amidst the challenges of these new, yet unformed, communities.

Those workers and leaders from the public sector who helped us with our research expressed negative feelings about their work and some dejection and loss of morale. Yet they retained a very positive desire to make a difference to people's lives by making their services work. Most interviewees concluded their contribution by expressing enthusiasm and a sense of being energized by the work that they do, or even joy. Ultimately their confidence in what they do is boosted by the people they serve. As one respondent put it, 'Seeing people increasing their skills, reaching new goals or being empowered to speak up are things that keep me doing what I do.' Despite the obvious challenges there is a huge pride in delivering effective services in these new urban areas.

References

Beresford, P., and Hoban, M., *Effective Participation in Anti-Poverty and Regeneration Work and Research*. Joseph Rowntree Foundation, York, 2005; available at <www.jrf.org.uk/knowledge/findings/socialpolicy/0395.asp>.

DETR (Department of the Environment, Transport and the Regions), *Our Towns and Cities. The Future: Delivering an Urban Renaissance – an Executive Summary*. HMSO, London, 2000.

NICE (National Institute for Health and Clinical Excellence), 'Lessons from Health Action Zones (Choosing Health? Briefing)', <www.nice.org.uk/aboutnice/whoweare/aboutthehda/hdapublications/lessons_from_health_action_zones_choosing_health_briefing.jsp> (accessed 25 June 2008).

Putnam, R., *Bowling Alone: The Collapse and Revival of American Community*. Simon and Schuster, New York, 2000.

Todorovic, J., and Wellington, S., *Living in Urban England: Attitudes and Aspirations*. Department of the Environment, Transport and the Regions, London, 2000.

Wilkinson, D., and Appelbee, E., *Implementing Holistic Government: Joined-Up Action on the Ground*. Policy Press, Bristol, 1999.

6

The wider perspective: the Church in the new urban developments

Those who are studying urban areas from a global perspective are aware that new types of built environment are emerging and new styles of development are appearing within cities and on their suburban peripheries. Having heard in earlier chapters the voices of those experiencing the new developments in the south-east of England and specifically in the Thames Gateway, we now step back for a moment and broaden our focus for a while to other countries and other parts of Britain so that we can better appreciate the nature of the changes taking place. We will also begin to reflect on the response of churches to the pastoral challenges and opportunities presented by these new peripheral areas, in anticipation of a closer look at church engagement in the Thames Gateway in Chapter 8.

The Durham Report, *Privatizing the City: The Tentative Push towards Edge Urban Developments and Gated Communities in the United Kingdom* (MacLeod 2004), locates its discussion of these new urban developments in the UK within the burgeoning global phenomenon of the edge city in the USA (of which there are roughly 200), and also around developing megacities such as São Paulo, Hong Kong, Johannesburg, Mumbai, Singapore, Manila and Jakarta. The Report is primarily a literature review and, as its title suggests, is a response to a perceived trend in housing demand in the UK which reflects a move to more privatized living and thus less public space. The key driver for this review was New Labour's concern with the sustainability agenda as defined by its report entitled *Sustainable Communities: Building for the Future* (ODPM 2003). This referred to the challenges to produce environmentally but also socially sustainable communities in the light of globalization and growing regional inequalities. It produced a list of sustainability criteria by which to measure and guide the development of new urban areas. Foremost among these criteria were:

- strong local leadership
- a flourishing local economy to provide jobs and wealth
- effective engagement and participation by local people
- a safe and healthy local environment.

The issue of sustainability (a broad and overarching concept) appears to have slipped down the political agenda, with the successor to the Office of the Deputy Prime Minister (ODPM), the Department of Communities and Local Government (DCLG), now focusing its policy priorities on specific targets related to social cohesion and diversity. However, it can be argued that sustainability is still an important theological and ethical concept which shapes the way that churches and other faith groups choose their priorities for engaging in new urban areas both within and outside the Thames Gateway.

As already mentioned, the Durham Report considers very carefully a new form of urban development which in the US is called 'edge cities'. A very large suburb grows up outside the parent city and becomes so substantial that it begins to take on a life independent of the local city. The people who live there find that, rather than face the long commute into the city each day, the area has grown so phenomenally that it caters for their every need – work, shops, schooling, accommodation and leisure. So 'successful' have some edge cities become that they are burgeoning at the expense of the parent city, which can even face decline as a consequence.

As we have already seen in Chapter 1, edge cities were first identified by the US commentator Joel Garreau (1991) and are created by a variety of economic, social and political forces. They partly emerge out of the neo-liberal economic agenda of the late 1980s, which stressed the need for business to expand unencumbered by the inefficiencies of public bureaucracies and congested city-centre locations, which were increasingly compromised by crumbling buildings and social infrastructure, poor transport networks, and high rents. Edge cities also emerge out of the dominance of the car culture and the diffusion of services that this dominance has generated in the form of highways, service stations, drive-through fast-food centres and out-of-town shopping malls. The physical spaces between these 'links', which 25 years ago were still deserted fields of 'corn stubble', are now expanding and joining up previously unconnected areas of land, consisting of housing mingled with service-sector and light-industry parks and low-rise 'college campus'-style HQs for computer or insurance companies, and are often located at major motorway intersections or adjacent to expanding airport hubs.

However, a growing literature from the United States also describes the downside to this type of urban lifestyle: stress brought on by excessive travelling, poor air quality leading to asthma and other respiratory diseases, increasing debt as house prices rise, poor public transport and other public services. Other commentators also observe a lack of any sense of community and history, and an absence of street life, social diversity and public space, which are necessary to nurture not only a feeling of belonging, but also a sense of well-being and security (see Jacobs 1992; Davis 1994; Layard 2005). This cluster of negative effects has led one US commentator to refer to the 'immiseration' of the middle classes (Soja 2000) – in other words, behind the successful façade of double garages and home-entertainment systems can lie a darker and hidden world of stress and loneliness.

The Durham Report points out that the UK (and indeed Europe in general) has yet to see the emergence of US-style independent stand-alone edge cities. A European study in 2002 (Phelps, McNeill and Parsons 2002) concluded that most of our edge urban spaces (e.g. Croydon) are the result of deliberate decentralization by government, rather than laissez-faire and immature political structures, and therefore European analysts prefer to use the term 'edge urban municipalities'. However, it is true to say that several areas in the UK share characteristics with their US and global counterparts in terms of design and function, and possibly social features as well.

The closest a UK city gets to the function and form of a US edge city is Milton Keynes, which falls within the gravitational pull of London (45 minutes away from central London by train). Milton Keynes has a network of high-speed dual carriageways which link discrete areas of low-density housing in the city, interspersed with light industry and service-sector and public-service employment hubs. At its heart is a huge regional shopping mall, which you would normally expect to find on the edge of a metropolis, with various other large retail and entertainment hubs dotted within its boundaries. Low-rise buildings sporadically appear above its generous provision of landscaped parkland and open areas, which are criss-crossed by pedestrian and cycle paths (locally known as redways) (see Charlesworth and Cochrane 1997; Baker 2005). In fact, Milton Keynes is a fully planned settlement built as a Mark 3 New Town under the provision of the 1947 New Towns Act.[1] Up until the late 1970s the area was only a vast swathe of low-level agricultural land in North Buckinghamshire interspersed with small villages.

Meanwhile many UK regional shopping centres have been built to a scale allowing the same level of amenities provided by small towns (e.g. railway and bus terminals, post offices, churches, cinemas, medical centres, banks). They then become the natural focus for surrounding residential development. We have examples of this all over the UK – the Metrocentre (Newcastle/Gateshead), Trafford Park (Manchester), Meadowhall (Sheffield), Merry Hill (West Midlands), Lakeside and Bluewater (South Essex and North Kent respectively), and Breahead (Glasgow).

Other 'edge-urban developments' that the Durham Report identifies are those emerging around motorway and airport hubs, including Bristol's North Fringe/Cribbs Causeway development, which has emerged along the M4/M5 intersection (and which will be described more fully in our specific case studies); the immediate Greater Manchester/Cheshire hinterland adjoining the M56 close to Manchester's expanding international airport; the new financial and IT hub called Edinburgh Park close to Edinburgh International Airport, which is projected to employ 12–15,000 people; the expansion of East and West Dunfermline and the expansion of Inverness as the hub city for the Northern Highlands and Western Isles (with the possible planning of a new town of 60,000 close by).

So whilst the UK has only a very few towns or cities which rival US developments for the name of 'edge city', expanding hubs of new urban development are emerging across the UK. Various terms have been used to describe them, such as 'exurban' or 'edge-urban devel-

---

[1] Mark 3 New Towns were the new 'super-towns', such as Telford and Milton Keynes, designed in the late 1960s and built in the mid- to late 1970s for populations of up to 250,000.

opments', but their variety and the more closely packed nature of the British urban landscape makes them look significantly different. As one new British urban development grows into the next, a term more appropriate to much of our new-built urban space might better be 'edgeless cities' – at present we do not see many bold, 'stand-alone' edge cities as in the US. Nevertheless, this type of development is spreading so rapidly in today's globally financed world that we might expect the unexpected any day.

Three case studies of church-based engagement

Thus far we have focused our attention on the communities at large in the new urban areas, but now we home in on the churches to learn how they view these developments and how they have thus far sought to respond to them. We therefore examine the experiences of church-based communities working in a variety of edge-urban locations across Britain (ranging from less than five years old to 20). A number of church-based and non-church-based members from each community were asked the following four questions:

1 How would you describe the types of people who are living or have recently moved into your area?
2 How would you describe the main features of their lifestyle?
3 How would you describe the main concerns and priorities of those living in your area?
4 How would you describe the challenges and opportunities that you face in engaging with your new communities?

This last question tended to be followed up by questions along the lines of:

(a) Where are the points of contact?
(b) How receptive are they to ideas of 'church'?

We begin each case study with a brief description of the area before examining the Church's response and engagement.

Cambourne, Cambridgeshire
Context and profile

Cambourne is situated eight miles west of Cambridge on the edge of the busy A428, which connects it to Milton Keynes, and is close to the A1 and M11. It is a planned development of approximately 4,000 homes (or 12,000 people) which is still in the process of construction and was envisaged as a response to the overheated demand for housing in the Cambridge area; other housing growth areas around the Cambridge perimeter – which are being developed, however, by adding to existing settlements – include Long Stanton, Northfield and Trumpington. The development of Cambourne started in 1999 and, to date, roughly 2,000 homes have been constructed with a current population of 5,000 new people. The demand for housing is so great that the developers have already negotiated an extra 700 homes to be added to the existing master plan (their original target was 1,500). Roughly 10 per cent of the housing is 'affordable housing' for rent. At Cambourne's heart is an 80-acre country park.

Thirty per cent of Cambourne's population are children aged up to 16, and 42 per cent are between 30 to 44. Less than 5 per cent are over 60. Nearly 17 per cent of the population define themselves as non-white British and in fact a total of 23 languages are spoken in the village (see CCC Research Group 2006), reflecting considerable ethnic diversity. There is little sign, however, of religious diversity, since of those in the survey of 800 who claimed some sort of religious practice, 92 per cent defined themselves as Christian. One of the main issues driving the life of this brand-new community is articulated by one church-based resident who describes the young professionals that make up the vast majority of the congregation as 'mortgaged to the hilt' (25 per cent are managers and senior officials, 24 per cent are in professional occupations and 21 per cent are associate professionals and technicians). In September 2007, one-bedroom apartments in Cambourne started at £150,000, going up to £550,000 for a six-bedroom detached house.

Cambourne residents also have high aspirations. Forty per cent of homeowners expressed the intention to move on within the next three years and 13 per cent were undecided, thus leaving only 47 per cent definitely saying they would stay more than three years. These last residents may mitigate some of the worst effects of population 'churn' identified by some of our interviewees. However, one interviewee mentioned that, while they are prepared to stay in Cambourne, the residents express a highly demanding attitude towards all service providers that borders on 'control-freakery'. They attribute this attitude to the framework of expectation raised by the almost Utopian terms in which Cambourne is sold to prospective residents as a stand-alone and distinctive community. Indeed, in surveys asking why people moved to Cambourne, it was the idea of moving to a 'village' that provided the strongest appeal (CCC Research Group 2006). However, the path from rhetoric to reality has not always been smooth. While the environment may be good in Cambourne, with large amounts of open space and lakes, social provision has lagged behind – often due to the complexity of the development arrangements and the desire to return a quick profit (involving at least three private developers). Many Section 106 provisions (community resources promised by developers as a result of planning gain) have yet to be met – including, crucially, a sports and leisure centre, seen as particularly important for a community with so many children and young people who need activity-based leisure facilities. However, the community success-fully lobbied for a church-controlled primary school (the second in the town), which is now in its third year of operation. It has no religious requirements for admission, but is described by one inter-viewee as 'an important offering to serve the whole community, especially in terms of future social sustainability'.

Promises of Utopian perfection come at a social and emotional cost. Some interviewees noted high levels of loneliness amongst some of the younger mums looking after children at home on their own. One informed us that the local doctors' surgery reports higher-than-average levels of depressive illness in Cambourne, reflected in the amount of time off work people seem to need. Although there are three buses an hour to Cambridge, there is also chronic depression amongst some of the population who have uprooted themselves from family networks and who feel a certain measure of alienation and isolation. This sense of alienation is expressed, perhaps surprisingly, in vandalism in the emerging town, which is attributed to youngsters growing up in an atmosphere of ano-nymity – the community 'boundaries and norms' which come with more mature social networks have yet to appear.

More positively, one interviewee with experience of working in British New Towns is complimentary about the relative hetero-geneity in the styles of housing, which compares favourably with what they term the 'uniformity and contemporary bleakness' of the New Town vernacular. The convenient infrastructure that has developed suits most people's mobile lifestyle – six eating places, one pub and a Morrison's café seem popular social hubs. Transport links are good and the environment is of high quality. However, the high social mobility, coupled with the still prohibitive cost of housing for first-time buyers, means a growing shift towards the buy-to-let market, which does raise questions about the long-term stability of some of Cambourne's areas, especially when we recall that less than half the current population intend staying more than three years.

Church engagement in Cambourne

The story behind the evolution of a church presence is inspirational. Starting roughly eight years ago in a double garage, the church moved into a room in a doctor's surgery before purchasing a pair of old mobile school classrooms with a grant from the district council. With a loan from the United Reformed Church, the local residents converted this into a temporary church, which at the time also did double duty as the only community facilities in the town. Church attendance grew to about 75. At the instigation of church members the Cambourne residents' association was also established. The church currently meets in the temporary community centre, called the Ark. A new church building is planned in a central space in the new High Street at a projected cost of £1.7 million, and will be jointly operated as a Church of England, Baptist, United Reformed Church and Methodist project.

The principles behind church engagement with the emerging community in Cambourne appear to be twofold: provide a meeting place for community events and other forms of social interaction, and then ask the question, 'How can we make something of this community?' This procedure could be characterized as a non-didactic, 'whole-person' approach to forming relationships, with the emphasis on positive welcome and affirmation in the hope that if and when an enquirer wants to raise serious issues of faith, the basis for a meaningful dialogue will already be laid. The town's only professional minister thus describes the mission statement of the church as simply 'Come and meet other people', and in the community centre where the church is temporarily based there is the opportunity to do this via yoga sessions, carers and tots groups, etc. It seems as though a slightly paradoxical 'strategic way of being' – or a 'purposeful background presence' – are the concepts informing this type of approach to mission and ministry. Offering choice also appears to be important. There are two types of main Sunday liturgy on offer – one service offers a sense of tradition and reflectiveness, the other is much more contemporary and inter- active. The minister stresses that these services are not marketed for any age or denominational profile, since people often enjoy both and do not fit normal expectations. Meanwhile the experience of gathered Christian community is also offered at a variety of other time slots and locations – school, homes, the community centre and outside events such as community picnics or rambles. The minis- ter reflects that the Church exists to respond to those existential questions which are often prompted by the upheaval of moving into a new community – it is often a 'turbulent time' and the Church has the positive opportunity to be alongside people at this key life stage, helping them make sense of their deeper and more problem- atic human experiences.

North Bristol: Bradley Stoke
Context and profile

Bradley Stoke is a large housing development (roughly 25,000 resi- dents) built in the last 20 years around the intersection of the M4 and M5 motorways north of Bristol (known as the North Fringe). As we have already noted, the key difference between US and European 'edge developments' is that the latter are usually created by predetermined regional or national strategies for dealing with excess housing demand or economic growth. Back in the 1970s Avon County Council recognized the need to compensate for the decline in manufacturing employment elsewhere in the Bristol city region and identified this agricultural site near the motorways as a suitable case for development. However, it wasn't until the late 1980s that building work started.

The main drivers for housing growth have been the development of the Aztec West business park, which currently employs 5,000 in 86 companies; a second business park, Almondsbury Park; the devel- opment of Parkway North as a mixed site featuring hypermarket, retail and warehouse outlets; and the Abbey Wood site, which is occupied by the Ministry of Defence Procurement Division – 1.2

million square feet of purpose-built office space with an employment capacity of 6,000.

Bradley Stoke is populated primarily by white-collar workers who, as well as working in Bristol (Orange Telecommunications, the Ministry of Defence, Hewlett-Packard, RAC, Rolls Royce, BAE), also commute to Swindon, South Wales and London. The town's own Wikipedia entry (Wikipedia 2008) is perhaps less than flattering. During the housing slump of the 1990s it was locally nicknamed 'Sadly Broke' due to the rising negative equity in the area. The Wikipedia entry also comments that the town has 'become synonymous with large-scale, soulless housing developments, albeit without the social problems historically experienced by many older estates'. One interviewee who lives and works in the community reinforces this view by claiming that there is still no real centre to Bradley Stoke (in a social sense, at least). There is a large Tesco store, soon to be upgraded to a hypermarket, but no other range of shops to choose from. The town's first secondary school was completed only recently – the town also has sports facilities and a library building. The main problems identified, apart from a lack of diversity within the shopping environment, were traffic congestion (there is a serious lack of public transport – a proposed metro/tram system has been shelved for the time being) and an absence of facilities for young people (80 per cent of the population is under 40). One interviewee reports quite high levels of single-parent families due to the break-up of relationships, and although there are a number of public spaces in Bradley Stoke, the overall feel is that of a privatized community with people accessing forms of community elsewhere in the Bristol region.

This idea of 'passing through' space on the way to another destination is reinforced by the thumbnail sketches drawn of the residents of Bradley Stoke by our interviewees. In the view of those we interviewed, 'materialism' is the driving feature of daily life, 'holidays, quality of homes, replacing the three-piece suite and acquiring the latest telly'. The residents dress 'fairly well – take regular holidays', but the overall effect is that of privatized space – lots of individuals and self-contained families whose lives are spent with both partners working overtime and meeting the pressure of deadlines. 'Life is full up with work – there is not much space for much else.' Indeed the Bristol *Evening Post* has run a series of articles on the apparent lack of neighbourliness in Bradley Stoke, dubbing it the community 'where no one knows their neighbour'. One interviewee tells the story of a friend who lives in the development but whose family lives outside the Northern Fringe and whom he sees only at weekends. He uses his house as a revolving door – a place 'where he can almost "re-set himself" before going out again'. The interviewee continues, 'Peoples' social contacts have nothing to do with where they live – they are mainly found in work environments', and comments that the lack of family life in the community means there is as yet no established sense of social continuity. Many of those who have bought houses are highly mobile – 'they have been sent to work in Bristol because of promotion and will be sent on again – so there is a relatively high turnover of people'. They work long hours, so in the evening they tend, in the words of one of our interviewees, to 'crash out' at home and 'shut themselves away with their families'.

However, our interviewees did detect the beginning of the establishment of community, with increasing numbers of older people (i.e. those over 50) considering Bradley Stoke their home. There are now monthly fresh produce stalls and a monthly community magazine, and it seems that many residents are happy with what Bradley Stoke provides, which is essentially mobility and the opportunity to invest in their home.

Church engagement in Bradley Stoke

Within Bradley Stoke, the above-average number of young families means that rites of passage, particularly baptism, form a major part of the strategy to connect with embryonic communities. Baptism visits offer a bridge into the concerns and aspirations of young families facing the sort of pressures outlined above by allowing discussion to be edged towards 'what we think is important'. As one clergyperson we interviewed says, 'One of the cutting edges of the gospel is that we are an open community', and this openness translates itself into a programme of social events – 'the invitation to come and join something' is a tangible expression of that commitment to an open form of hospitality. For example, among the successful social bridges that have been built is a series of open camping weekend socials, supplemented by Alpha courses, intensive 'mums and tots work', intensive schools work, including the children's Christmas party, which attracted over 150 children, and a monthly 'open-ended' service that is based on 'coffee tables and asking questions'. In other words, the emphasis is on providing top-quality (what one of our interviewees calls 'decent') social events that model alternative, possibly counter-cultural, values of community and hospitality (within a prevailing ethos of overwork, mobility and retreat into privatized home space) whilst at the same time offering an open, non-didactic space for the opportunities to ask deeper, gospel-shaped questions about the meanings and priorities of life.

A recent private internal audit of life in one of Bradley Stoke's churches, based on Robert Warren's book *The Healthy Churches' Handbook* (Warren 2004), emphasized the importance of looking outward by means of an ever-improving menu of social events. This menu is not an end in itself, but an expression of part of what one church leader calls 'whole-life discipleship' – in other words, the church in Bradley Stoke needs to be committed to nurturing the life of the community from Monday to Saturday, as much as focusing on what happens on a Sunday morning.

The emphasis on children's and young people's work in Bradley Stoke, with its higher proportion of teenagers, is reflected and conducted through the local schools (as the important social hubs of nascent settlements) as well as a team of church-based youth workers involved in both church-centred and outreach activities. The clergy team report that they are 'blessed with a brilliant community building', in which the liturgical space is just one component which allows a 'community crossover into the church'. This building is open seven days a week and, as well as offering the usual menu of educational and social activities for the whole community, also functions as a democratic and 'public space' hub. The community building, for example, was the only space where those standing for local and parliamentary elections could participate in church-sponsored pre-election debates. The centre was also used as a polling station.

However, one interviewee reported that a growing emphasis on church-sponsored youth work could mean the church is in danger of missing the increasingly hard-to-reach group of the over-fifties. This growing section of the community typically reflects a second generation of residents who don't come from a church family and who are comfortably well off, and are therefore asking, 'Why do I need to go to church?'

The main strategy of the ecumenically based Bradley Stoke church is therefore to engage as much as possible with those within the community who use the building. This means that the church can rely on a more natural 'crossover' to generate new recruitment and ongoing levels of support. However, although the Bradley Stoke church is continuing to see a modest growth in its congregation (membership is currently around 60 adults and 30 children), a church member reflects that a breakthrough into more active representation and greater impact within the wider community is hampered by what they define as endemic 'apathy towards things religious', coupled with extreme 'busyness', as well as erratic attendance from those who would define themselves as committed Christians and churchgoers. So a typical level of attendance might be 'once or twice a month' – the other Sundays being absorbed by 'shopping, sport (typically children's sporting clubs) or visiting family'.

Meanwhile, another member articulately reflects on the wider challenge of being church in the consumerist, postmodern environment that is not unique to Bradley Stoke, but which, because it is still a relatively new community, they feel has its own 'Bradley Stoke twist': 'It is the atmosphere of the whole country which is anti-religious. Christianity is perceived as something "historic" – not for now. The media has played up the impact of Richard Dawkins and *The Da Vinci Code* – it is not so much a direct challenge, more a popular perception of irrelevance or sensationalism that has filtered into the atmosphere.'

East Dunfermline

Context and profile

Our third UK edge-urban case study emerges from the housing hotspot developing on the eastern flanks of the former small industrial town of Dunfermline across the Firth of Forth from Edinburgh. Following de-industrialization in the post-war period, the fortunes of the town were revived in the 1980s and '90s with the attraction of global technology and communications firms such as Hyundai and Motorola. While the subsequent bursting of the 'dot.com bubble' meant further unemployment as microchip factories were closed, the overheating of the Edinburgh housing market has in turn created the demand for new housing outside its boundaries and allowed for the growth of the service sector, with financial and media industries established in Dunfermline (e.g. Halifax Bank of Scotland and BSkyB). This has led to demand for up to 4,500 new houses on Dunfermline's eastern flank and increased transport links (for example, the extension of the railway line to Alloa). Meanwhile, a new leisure and entertainment hub called Fife Leisure Park has also been built adjacent to junction 3 of the M90 (on the northern edge of the eastern flank). It contains a ten-screen multiplex cinema, bingo hall, bowling alley and gym, as well as fast-food restaurants and a new hotel.

According to one professional interviewee living and working in the area, the first wave of housing, in the eastern area of expansion, was high-quality homes for residents who were keen to move to a semi-rural setting. Subsequent waves have seen the development of cheaper, higher-density housing, which is attracting a considerable influx of immigrants beyond the Fife and Lothian areas of Scotland – English, South Africans, Eastern Europeans, and a significant number of immigrants from other African nations such as Ghana and the Indian subcontinent. This means that the new parts of East Dunfermline are much more cosmopolitan than the old town. The average age of the new residents is the early thirties, and they are employed at mid-management level in the new industries described above, or else self-employed within one of the support industries attached to major firms in the area. According to local church sources, the new residents of East Dunfermline fit a cultural and employment profile that is now becoming familiar: 'Two parents, 1.5 children, two cars and a caravan, commuter dormitory, Tescoville', is one commendably concise summary of the prevailing 'feel' of this development area, along with the observation that its residents are time-poor (on average, two to three hours a day are spent commuting to and fro across the increasingly 'clogged up' Firth of Forth bridge, which is struggling to deal with increased commuter flows at peak times). Nevertheless, disposable incomes are relatively high. This income is invested mainly in home entertainment systems (broadband connection rates are very high in this part of the parish).

However, a deeper and possibly darker analysis of the lifestyle behind this headline characterization emerges from other observations offered by the churchpeople living in the midst of this new community. These cluster around health issues such as stress, excessive weight (often linked to high cholesterol levels), sleeplessness ('People here never seem to switch off') and high levels of alcohol consumption in the home – although this may be partly due to the lack of pubs in this new area of Dunfermline. Other interviewees voice the familiar refrain concerning the importance of 'keeping up with the Joneses and the ways in which personal identity seems to be perhaps over-dependent on being seen to have the latest car, or dressing your children in the right designer labels'. One person offered the reflection that this might be linked to the fact that, in a new community, no one knows their neighbours and so there is no way of forming an in-depth opinion of your neighbour's accomplishments or values. Therefore residents in new communities might need to rely on 'semiotics' to convey to each other their own sense of who they are and what they have achieved.

With regard to relationships, one respondent offered the opinion that new residents did not appear 'to see the use of relating on a convivial basis'. Rather, 'there is a fundamentalist individualism – and an insufficient mutuality', partly attributed, according to this interviewee, to the fact that the 50 per cent or so of those who have moved into East Dunfermline from existing areas of Fife or Lothian still see their old communities (only 10 or 15 miles away) as the main locus of their cultural identity.

Other interesting anecdotes also emerge in relation to the issues of community formation in these nascent edge-urban developments. One church interviewee spoke of taking her courage in her hands in order to meet what she perceived as the social deficit in the community. She started a coffee morning and was amazed at the ease with which word got around and at the enthusiasm of other women for these meetings. Another interviewee reflected on the extent to which the rhythm of East Dunfermline life is set by the commuting agenda. As an occasional home-worker, he observes 'the hordes leaving at 7.30 in the morning and returning at 6.30 in the evening,' and concludes, 'I could walk up and down the street naked at lunchtime and nobody would be here to notice – that's how empty it is.'

Finally, one observation that emerges from East Dunfermline more strongly than from our other case studies concerns the lack of mature democratic structures within the area. Institutional bureaucracies such as local authorities (and even churches) can struggle to recognize nascent networks within new communities (especially those that emerge instead of being strategically planned). Residents therefore come to believe that the needs of the community are not being taken seriously by local political structures. This is reflected in the delays in provision of adequate community and educational facilities, a delay exacerbated, in the residents' opinion, by the reliance on Private Finance Initiatives to supply much of this social infrastructure. The lack of buildings with a community focus has made it difficult for the channelling and articulation of political demands from these new and increasingly disparate communities. Reliance on fly-posting generates only fleeting political interest. Meanwhile, the Church of Scotland has struggled to negotiate with a local council, whose approach to governance is, in the opinion of one resident, 'as secular as France', for an affordable plot of land on which to build a church. Currently it meets in the local school and in peoples' houses – but the local authority has persistently refused to allow the church to use any public buildings.

On a more positive note, many residents commented on the ease of access to the cultural resources of a capital city such as Edinburgh, as well as easy access to the 'great outdoors'. There was also the obvious attraction of 'getting more for your money' on a house purchase, especially garden space.

Church engagement in East Dunfermline

The overall impression of church engagement within this Scottish edge-urban development is one of excitement but also challenge. The feeling of the leadership of this nascent Church of Scotland community (currently around 40 adults and 20 children) is that the wider community 'can't see the need for church', for many of the reasons outlined above. Indeed, one leader says that this church community doesn't yet act like an established church – more like 'a tentative set of relationships'. The church is therefore required to adopt a strategy, according to another congregational member, of 'penetrating' what networks exist within the community 'by proxy' – that is, organizing local events, such as a community carnival, that tap into the desire for a depth of relationship that also affirms one's existing lifestyle. As we have already seen with church strategy in other areas, this primarily involves investing heavily in schools and youth work via holiday clubs (including, in this case, a travelling fun bus) and a women's social group open to all women but run by Christians. Since the church currently meets in a local school, there is perhaps a natural crossover between the emerging church and families with children of primary school age. Elsewhere, there are 'network' groups meeting in members' houses for Bible study.

A number of further observations from our respondents flesh out a bit more some of the small but significant dynamics that affect church-based work in these new urban communities. First was the reflection that despite the considerable investment from the church in meeting the wider community within the emerging networks of the area, and indeed in creating its own networks, potential church members are still reticent to 'take the next step and become a faith community'. One church leader describes much of their church activity as a form of 'pre-evangelism'. It is perhaps evidence of the more demanding conditions in which new church communities now have to work that, at present, much of this pre-evangelistic activity (i.e. establishing relationships and patterns of interaction with either busy, apathetic or sceptical neighbours) appears to be reaping meagre returns.

Second, those within the new communities most susceptible to engaging with the church community are not 'local immigrants' but those from more global contexts.

Third, in some of the reflections there was an implicit sense that older and more established members of the churches in these new areas (perhaps those over sixty) struggle to understand or support what they see as woolly forms of mission engagement. One such interviewee commented that whilst they endorsed the overall approach of creating 'a space where everyone can come', they felt there was a danger of producing a 'wishy-washy' or 'dumbed-down' version of Christianity in order to get people in church: 'People get quite taken aback when the church wants to be more hard-hitting.' This means that in their early phase, church communities can, in the words of another interviewee, 'fall in between a number of stools' – not traditional enough for the older and more committed members that one needs in order to create the core community, but also perhaps running the risk that what is designed as 'pre-evangelism', or using 'networks as proxy', is not distinctive enough to challenge engrained attitudes and behaviour which 'sees no need for church'.

Fourth, the church in East Dunfermline is clear that in its community outreach it must challenge the implicit 'social apartheid' that exists between the first wave of incomers (living in high-end, executive housing) and subsequent waves who live in either more affordable or social housing. In other words, this church community has rightly recognized the exclusion and marginalization that flourishes even within these apparently homogeneous and comfortable settlements.

Finally, the website of this church community is a particularly well-maintained, attractive and easy-to-use portal, with an emphasis on e-mail enquiry as an initial step into further interaction. It makes use of generally holistic spiritual images (pebbles on a beach, sunflowers and so on) and a wide range of non-Christian quotes on banner headlines under each section on the website – including the Buddha, Albert Einstein and Gladiator.

Conclusions

In conclusion, we can now start to identify some overlapping experiences and issues relating to how new church communities engage in mission within edge-urban developments.

The different ways in which church-based people perceive their fellow-residents in these developments begin to crystallize as follows:

- They see them as time-poor but often materially comfortable.
- The home is the sanctuary from the stress of overwork, usually expressed in home entertainment, home improvements and domestic alcohol consumption.
- Hypermarkets and entertainment nodes suggest convenience and homogeneity – a space to pass through rather than engage with.
- There is stress caused by hypermobility (e.g. too much travel) and meeting debt/mortgage repayments, as evidenced in the way people eat, sleep and possibly conduct relationships.

- There is a heavy preponderance of young families and children, who in some of the slightly older developments have now become teenagers – with a lack of facilities for them.
- Surprisingly high levels of ethnic diversity are to be found within many new urban areas, although not necessarily religious diversity.
- Low political capital can help reinforce a sense that these areas are more private than public spaces.
- Schools are the natural social hubs for these areas.
- Loneliness and lack of close support networks have been observed, especially for young parents 'stuck at home' with young families.
- Religious literacy appears low, and there is not much sense of common norms and values, which tend to be associated with more mature communities.

In response to this social and cultural profile, the churches we spoke to seem to have commonly adopted the following mission principles and praxis:

- an emphasis on social events that build bridges or connect to emerging networks in order to help reinforce a sense of community and hospitality;
- an emphasis on schools, children's and youth work;
- an open, person-centred approach to faith that creates spaces for asking questions, rather than a formalized, didactic approach;
- a wide variety of different liturgical events at points of natural contact with the wider community;
- the extensive use of websites and e-mail communication to provide a portal for the wider community, including the use of holistic images and messages alongside specifically Christian imagery;
- the holding of mass events but also the use of smaller and more informal networks.

We began this survey with a reminder of the government's political priority concerning the importance of creating 'sustainable communities', in both the environmental and political, economic and social sense. The issue of social sustainability is particularly acute given the emergence of new edge-urban communities on a hitherto unprecedented scale – not only in the Thames Gateway, but in other UK hotspots as well. At the heart of the emerging church-based methods we have uncovered is the attempt to create flexible yet sustainable ecclesial communities at the core of new urban spaces. The familiar narratives on which sociality in more traditional communities was built – those of common experience, generational stability, recognition of neighbour, common values and norms, a sense of collective identity – have now apparently been stripped away by the mobility and privatism these new urban spaces appear to epitomize. We need more time, probably a minimum of 20 years, to tell whether these church-based attempts at creating sustainable communities will be successful.

References

Baker, C., 'Religious Faith in the Exurban Community – A Case Study of Christian Faith-Communities in Milton Keynes', *City*, 9(1) (April 2005): pp. 109–24.

CCC (Cambridgeshire County Council) Research Group, *Living in Cambourne – A Survey of Cambourne Residents*. CCC Research Group, Cambridge, 2006.

Charlesworth, J., and Cochrane, A., 'Anglicising the American Dream: Tragedy, Farce and the "Post-Modern" City', in S. Westwood and J. Williams (eds), *Imagining Cities*. Routledge, London, 1997.

Davis, M., 'The Suburban Nightmare: While Older Suburbs Experience Many Problems of the Inner City, "Edge Cities" Now Offer a New Escape', *Los Angeles Times*, 23 October 1994.

Garreau, J., *Edge City: Life on the New Frontier*. Doubleday, New York, 1991.

Jacobs, J., *The Death and Life of Great American Cities*. Vintage Books, New York, 1992.

Layard, R., *Happiness: Lessons from the New Science*. Penguin, London, 2005.

MacLeod, G., *Privatizing the City? The Tentative Push towards Edge Urban Developments and Gated Communities in the United Kingdom*. International Centre for Regional Regeneration and Development Studies, University of Durham, 2004.

ODPM (Office of the Deputy Prime Minister), *Sustainable Communities: Building for the Future*. ODPM, Wetherby, 2003.

Phelps, N., McNeill, D., and Parsons, N., 'In Search of a European Edge Identity: Trans-European Networking among Edge Urban Municipalities', *European Urban and Regional Studies*, 9 (2002): pp. 211–24.

The wider perspective: the Church in the new urban developments

Soja, E., *Postmetropolis*. Blackwell, Oxford, 2000.

Warren, R., *The Healthy Churches' Handbook: A Process for Revitalizing your Church*. Church House, London, 2004.

Wikipedia, 'Bradly Stoke', <http://en.wikipedia.org/wiki/Bradley_Stoke> (accessed 17 June 2008).

7

Gaining theological perspective

And I saw the holy city, the new Jerusalem, coming down out of heaven from God, prepared as a bride adorned for her husband. And I heard a loud voice from the throne saying,

'See, the home of God is among mortals.
He will dwell with them;
they will be his peoples,
and God himself will be with them;
he will wipe every tear from their eyes.'

(Revelation 21.2–4a)

'As Christians, we hope for eternity. But eternity is not what happens at the end of time, when we are dead. It begins now, whenever we share God's life. It breaks in whenever we overcome hatred with love' (Radcliffe 2007: 22). These words of the Dominican friar Timothy Radcliffe are a reminder that Christians are people of hope and promise, not merely people of optimism, and what's more that hope is sampled now.

Christians have the opportunity to enjoy a relationship with their creator and redeemer in order to embrace, for themselves and for others, the abundance of life offered in the gospel – sampled now but enjoyed in full later. Under the guidance and judgement of these fundamentals, this chapter uses imagery from the book of Revelation, especially its climax of the 'New Jerusalem', clustering some of the observations and comments emerging from the reflections and conversations earlier in the book around a number of theological themes which focus upon human flourishing.

Babylon: the city of endless desire

In his book *Cities of God*, Graham Ward argues that cities are symbols of civilization and culture embodying a relationship between the personal, social and cosmic orders.

The emerging new cities and urban areas, argues Ward, move away from cities whose architecture embodies 'eternal aspiration' to those embodying 'endless desire'. At a time when retail therapy is recognized as not merely a hobby but almost a defining element of post-modern life, modern cities provide the allurements and attractions of 'endless desire'. Here is embodied the core dynamic of consumerism, which says that in order to 'be', it is necessary to 'have'. Great malls like Meadowhall in Sheffield or Bluewater in Kent, the latter described not simply as a shopping mall but as a shopping and leisure destination, are the modern cathedrals of today. Ward writes, 'In the collapse of the modern city, Disneyland simulacra take over. The new industries are the leisure industries thriving in and fostering a culture of seduction, a culture of euphoric grasping of the present in order to forget the present, submerge it in a wet dream or a massive surge of adrenalin. It is this culture of seduction which Christian theology has to respond to' (Ward 2000: 68).

As Chapter 1 has pointed out, if endless desire is the Utopia driving the new urban developments, then a theological response needs to offer a Christian understanding of right desire – the desire of God for humanity and humanity's desire for communion with God and with other human beings. Looking and listening lie at the heart of qualitative mission. The task of this chapter, therefore, is to reflect on the careful looking and listening attempted in the foregoing chapters so as to engage with the post-modern city and culture in a way which is creative, positive and critical. We will do so inevitably and rightly with minds and hearts shaped by the Christian tradition and our own context. We must look at and listen to the Gateway in order to weave the fabric of the Christian tradition into this new urban context so that all involved can get in touch with the creator who gives meaning to existence. In this encounter both tradition and contemporary context can be renewed and transformed.

In considering the Gateway, two caveats need to be borne in mind. First, the Thames Gateway is made up of so many different communities and 'villages' that it should not be regarded as homogeneous. Although communities across the Gateway have much in common, such as their cultural climate, they are socially diverse. Newcomers in the Gateway north of the Thames face different issues from those in Kent Thameside; existing communities in Kent Thameside, because of the nature of their location, are affected by regeneration in ways different from those in other parts of the Gateway. This mixture of characteristics produces a mixture of identities. Second, this chapter, like the book as a whole, is not a systematic treatise but an attempt to explore the interface between theology and context in the hope that something new will emerge either in the writing or the reading. Sculptor Anthony Carro encourages those viewing his work to go inside and under the metal bars and girders in order to experience the various shapes and patterns, thereby seeing the world, themselves and his art from new and different perspectives. That is the aim of this chapter.

Utopia or the New Jerusalem?

Utopia means, literally, 'No Place', although an alternative spelling, 'Eutopia' (literally 'Good Place'), later endowed the same word with a positive meaning. However, as 'No Place' does not exist and at its best is unreachable, Utopia is the product of optimism rather than of hope. Optimism yearns for the best based on fear of failure. Hope looks forward to the best, on the basis that the promises of God are already being sampled. Whilst Plato's Utopian vision of society and Thomas More's Utopia never existed and were therefore never accessible, today 'Utopia' is a popular game on the Web describing itself as a medieval fantasy game, 'the world's most popular interactive game'. The Utopia game allows you to create your own world on the Web, to spend as much time as you want in it and to make and meet your own friends according to your own choice. This is reminiscent of the beliefs that the future is to be produced and managed, and that it is not God's Kingdom or the saints' communion but humanity's Utopia that is more realizable.

There has been an array of Utopian visions for the Thames Gateway. For example, Medway Council drew upon the expertise of Alfonso Martinez Cearra, who was responsible for the redevelopment plans in Bilbao in northern Spain. Cearra's five basic points which undergird city regeneration are: (1) build on values, not projects; (2) make culture central to your values; (3) support leaders and visionaries; (4) build the future from the past; and finally, (5) bring your dreams with you. It is interesting, therefore, for Christians to reflect on the values which come from a different culture and context – the Christian scriptural culture.

The book of Revelation was written for Christians living in a climate of uncertainty and persecution. The Roman Empire was venting its spleen upon the alternative culture of the embryonic Christian community. The author, John, is concerned that some of his audience is compromising too much with the 'global' cultural values of the Roman Empire, while he wants to comfort and encourage others in the midst of the difficulties they are facing. John's theological method is to lift their sights onto a wider and higher plane by showing them a vision which will bring inspiration, encouragement and challenge in their daily lives. It is important to note that unlike the 'Utopia' game, John's Revelation does not provide his readers with an escape route into another world, but uses otherworldly imagery to bring them back into this world by showing what forces are at work in human history and how human beings and human institutions are being manipulated by those forces. Justice and redemption are deep concerns of John, and although they will not be finally realized until 'the kingdom of the world has become the kingdom of our Lord and of his Messiah' (Revelation 11.15), it is important for followers of Christ to work with those values here and now.

The final vision in the book of Revelation (chs 21—22) is about heaven coming down to earth in order to sanctify it. Eugene Peterson puts it this way:

> Many people want to go to heaven the way they want to go to Florida – they think the weather will be an improvement and the people decent. But the biblical heaven is not a nice environment far removed from the stress of hard city life. It is the invasion of the city by the City. We enter heaven not by escaping what we don't like but by the sanctification of the place in which God has placed us. This is not a long (eternal) weekend away from responsibilities of employment and citizenship, but the intensification and healing of them. (Peterson 1988: 174)

In order to encourage, support and challenge his late-first-century readers, John provides a picture of the New Jerusalem, which is a glimpse of God's realized future, and he uses language and symbolism which would have resonated powerfully and deeply with his readers. Christian theology teaches that creation is moving towards an end-time, an 'eschatological' time, when the earth will be under the rule of the Kingdom of God. In Jesus Christ, a foretaste of life in God's Kingdom is provided, for example, when love and concern is shown to the poor and marginalized. Christians are called to live out the Kingdom in this world, as far as they are able, so that they can enjoy it to the full when they come to God's Kingdom. It therefore follows that Christians need to shape the communities around them in new urban areas so that they can be a foretaste of God's eschatological Kingdom.

Community and belonging

If men and women are going to embrace life in today's new urban areas, they need to feel at home and that they belong. But the pictures in the Gateway planning of what community might mean are blurred and haphazard. It appears that creating community, while part of the Gateway's Utopian vision, has not figured highly in the delivery.

While newcomers are excited about their new homes and new possibilities, interviews with people in existing communities suggest they are frustrated by their inability to shape the new communities, and they soon share with the new arrivals a lack of confidence in the authorities to provide for community needs. Both newcomers and existing residents are increasingly alienated from the decisions and policies carried out in the Gateway because of a dearth of consultation, and so they lose faith in the democratic process – a problem in society as a whole. Even though there has been local consultation on a number of occasions, the existing communities do not believe that their voices were heard, still less acted upon. What comes across in many interviews in Chapters 2 and 3, reinforced by observations in Chapter 4, is that, while there may have been a nod in the direction of consultation, there was the suspicion that decisions had already been made even before the consultation was held. Furthermore, when new communities are built alongside older communities, such as in Kent Thameside, little effort appears to be made to integrate the new with the old and the commercial interests of developers hold sway. This is manifest, for example, in the way that Fastrack, the rapid bus service with dedicated lanes, has developed in Northfleet (see pp. 72–3).

While newcomers are not thinking of the Gateway as a permanent home (though this does not preclude the possibility that it will become permanent), people living in existing communities, and who have deep roots there, do not see themselves moving as a result of the redevelopment around them. There is frequently ambivalence toward and even resentment against new residents, but people whose family have grown up in the area and whose loved ones have died in the area tend to be committed to staying. Some will remain until they die – 'The only way I'll leave this place is in a box,' said one resident – whereas others will stay as long as they can manage on their own.

An African woman who has lived in ethnically mixed North Woolwich for 24 years expressed a view in Chapter 2 that was not unrepresentative of the long-stay African and Caribbean community. She did not feel as though she belonged to the community (she was happy when she had closed the door of her flat), but she had a strong sense of belonging to the Church. But apart from church members, she does not have other friends in the community. She looked back with nostalgia to the village community in Africa from which she came, commenting that the people there do not have very much, but they value what they do have. She hoped that in the long term she would share her time between the UK and Africa. A Nigerian woman from a similar background, also interviewed in Chapter 2 and who has spent 27 years in Canning Town but is happy living in the community, indicated that when she retires she would like to share her time between Nigeria and the UK: 'I go to work, I sleep, I cook, I shop and I come to church. Yes, I suppose you could say my life is here. But my heart is in Africa.'

However, the community is more than neighbourhood relationships. The communities pictured in the Hebrew Scriptures and the New Testament are more dynamic and inspirational than that. They show us that a healthy community needs to have in the present a dynamic relationship with the past and with the future. This volume has described many examples of people struggling for, and working on, community in the present. We have seen the significance of the past for community where cherished memories and departed loved ones are holding people in an area when all else appears gloomy. The search for shared history and common myths gives another indication of the importance of the past for a community. In

Chafford Hundred the discovery, during the building, of a World War II plane and the body of a US airman preserved in the clay caused a flurry of excitement as these events held out the possibility of historical roots and a community story. The oast house design of Bluewater shopping mall in Kent Thameside and its internal sculpture and art are attempts to link this edifice, built in a disused chalk pit, with the past. Similarly, the importance of a link with the future for the well-being of community is seen in the way that people bemoan the fact that they have little or no say in the future development of their area.

The Christian Church has a lot of experience of creating, working with and reflecting upon community. God, as Father, Son and Holy Spirit, is community and, created in God's image, human beings cannot be fully human apart from community. The three persons of the Trinity are different from one another, and yet are indivisible, sharing equal power and authority yet being in mutually respectful relationships of profound love. Created in this image, human beings are made for relationships of this challenging quality. We are designed to work best in communities which respect differences, learn from them and celebrate them – sharing decision-making and power in a non-grasping but informed way so that the best gifts of each community participant can come to the fore. From religious communities to church communities, from cell groups to 'fresh expressions', from parish level to the Anglican Communion, Christians have experience of good, healthy communities and also of bad, dysfunctional communities. What Christians have discovered from the image of the New Jerusalem is that a community of perfect harmony will not be achieved in this world, but that the struggle for its justice and peace can be a pathway to better community. So our struggle to create community embodies our eschatological hope.

Eugene Peterson, commenting on chapters 2 and 3 of the book of Revelation, highlights the need for community in order to function as healthy human beings:

> Gospel is never for individuals but for a people. Sin fragments us, separates us and sentences us to solitary confinement. Gospel restores us, unites us and sets us in community. The life of faith revealed and nurtured in the biblical narratives is highly personal but never merely individual; always there is a family, a tribe, a nation – church. A believing community is the context for the life of faith. Love

cannot exist in isolation: away from others love bloats into pride. Grace cannot be received privately: cut off from others it is perverted into greed. Hope cannot develop in solitude: separated from the community, it goes to seed in the form of fantasies.

(Peterson 1988: 42–3)

Belonging, which is a fundamental element of community, depends primarily upon relationships within community, but these relationships can be reflected, shaped, helped and hindered by the built environment.

The dearth of open play space and free green community space in many of the new urban developments contradicts the promises in the glossy brochures used by estate agents to sell new properties. Our interviewees constantly lamented the lack of community buildings and sacred spaces which help to give an area a soul. The quality of building tells the residents if they have really been respected by the builders and developers. It helps them or hinders them from belonging.

In John's vision of the New Jerusalem, the richness of the built environment is significant:

> The wall is built of jasper, while the city is pure gold, clear as glass. The foundations of the wall of the city are adorned with every jewel; the first was jasper, the second sapphire, the third agate, the fourth emerald, the fifth onyx, the sixth cornelian, the seventh chrysolite, the eighth beryl, the ninth topaz, the tenth chrysoprase, the eleventh jacinth, the twelfth amethyst. And the twelve gates are twelve pearls, each of the gates is a single pearl, and the street of the city is pure gold, transparent as glass. (Revelation 21.18–21)

Yet even this can be regarded as a pale reflection of where the true wealth of the New Jerusalem lies. Wealth lies in relationships and the real jewel is the relationship between God and God's people. As God is with the people in the New Jerusalem, there is no need of a place of worship to mediate the relationship between God and his people: 'I saw no temple in the city, for its temple is the Lord God the Almighty and the Lamb' (Revelation 21.22). This verse speaks of a deep trust in a place, but this fundamental trust is fast disappearing from our societal relationships as the competitive and privatized ethos of the neo-liberal economy bites ever deeper into our culture.

There is of course a great deal of romantic nostalgia about the trusting relationships of former times, and for some older residents who are determined to stay against all the odds we noted that their rootedness often consists in memories of former relationships.

Community is not just about the present, but the present in a dynamic relationship with the past and the future. In Revelation the Lord God says, ' "I am the Alpha and the Omega," . . . who is and who was and who is to come, the Almighty' (Revelation 1.8). Throughout the Christian tradition is the understanding that God's present encompasses the past and the future, and this needs to be reflected in any community constructed by human beings. This has already been identified as a real challenge in areas without history or myth. In nomadic communities, the past was carried around in stories (narratives) and rituals and when nomadic communities became settled, their stories and rituals became embodied in buildings and artefacts. There need to be places, sacred and secular, available to each community where this story-telling and community-making can take shape. Often such places are established in older communities, but this is certainly not the case in many of the new communities with which we are concerned.

It is important to acknowledge, however, that before settlement the nomadic tribes still had a strong sense of shared identity and communal belonging. They had this without being rooted in one place. Similarly today, many will not feel the need of a geographical rootedness. They carry their community in their mobile phone and their relationships, through Facebook and YouTube, on the Web. The narrative which unites the actions of these mobile communities would appear to be the shared story of shopping, acquisition and leisure pursuits. If the nomads found a common tribal centre in the pilgrimage city, today's urban nomads congregate at the shopping malls – designed like cathedrals in many respects. Walter Brueggemann's scholarship has stressed how the Hebrew tribes yearned for a land of promise and how that became a treasured place for them as they developed their stories, traditions and liturgies related specifically to that land; and this has informed the Christian tradition of the importance of place for belonging. But our present mobile urban generation provokes the question as to whether community and belonging can indeed be founded upon relationships alone, without the necessity of place. This seems to go against the grain of our theological traditions, but our earlier stress on the doctrine of the Trinity has reminded us of the thoroughly dynamic nature of community. Perhaps the new mobile generation is a reinvention of the nomadic culture which will find a way of creating the stability necessary for human flourishing even without the requirement of static roots. Perhaps we will need to concentrate on the importance of 'belonging with' rather than 'belonging in'. This will have profound implications for the Church, her mission and her ecclesiology. Whilst for many, territory and shrine will remain paramount, there are many today who have lost all sense of roots, homeland, and even responsibility to the planet.

Finally, what promotes community cohesion? How can a local culture (or cultures) be encouraged and shaped? What turns space, be it geographical or relational, into place? The word 'culture' comes from the Latin word *colo*, which means worship. Formerly, a place of worship was central to community cohesion. In ancient cities, the place of worship was a mark of the civilization and culture and gave focus and centre to the community. In old villages, the church is to be found at the centre. Cathedral cities were designed so that the place of worship was at their heart. What temples, cathedrals and places of worship are at the heart of today's new urban areas? What provision is being made for places, signs and symbols which facilitate community cohesion?

We struggle to understand the true nature of the new urban developments. Are they a recapitulation of the old New Towns of the 1950s or is the edge city, or even the edgeless city, a new entity which requires new tools to describe and analyse it? Should today's new urban areas best be understood in contrast to the shanty towns of the megacities of the Southern Hemisphere – with the difference that whereas the latter look outside themselves for material resources but are self-sufficient in spiritual wealth, the former are self-sufficient in material wealth but look beyond themselves for spiritual resources?

Parts of the new British urban areas under consideration are expansions of older communities where social and communal infrastructures are already in place: they may need to be expanded or modified, but they are nevertheless in place. However, in other places, some yet to be built, little or no consideration appears to have been given to the social aspects of building communities.

Indeed, some of the houses are being built for a maximum of two occupants, which brings into sharp focus the dormitory as well as the temporary nature of occupancy. Near Ebbsfleet station in Kent, some newly built estates seem designed as convenient outposts for London commuters and for people without families. In certain Arab cities, such as Dubai, the authorities have decided that single people should not be allowed to occupy the residential areas at all because living singly is detrimental to community well-being. The same was true of the early colonial towns of America. Yet new urban areas are being designed expressly so that people can live alone.

In the Gateway, new communities are being built beside older and more traditional communities. In Kent Thameside, for example, new housing is being built in abandoned chalk pits from which it is possible to see older communities perched on a nearby hill. It is hoped that the two communities will complement each other, but it has often been the case (as we saw in Chapter 3) that resentment towards the new communities has issued in the hurling of missiles and firebombs at the new roofs from above the old quarry by disaffected gangs. The paradox is that barriers have been constructed between old and new communities. Often the newly built housing is specifically separated from the older, stigmatized community by gates or walls to increase the purchase price of the new housing. But could it be possible for the infrastructure (especially transport networks) to be designed and arranged in such a way that it looks towards the neighbouring longer-established areas to provide community and worship facilities? This would benefit newer and older communities, providing renewal for the latter and a wider vision for the former.

As we struggle to envision the development of community within the new urban areas, we are repeatedly struck by different aspects of Revelation's picture of the New Jerusalem.

Barriers and boundaries: salvation from outside the city walls

Of particular significance is that in the New Jerusalem the gates are pictured as always open, day and night (Revelation 21.25); and if the gates of the city are always open, presumably to enable people to come and go, then what is the purpose of the walls? When the gates are always open, city walls, originally built as defensive protection, take on another function. They no longer protect citizens from the outside and they no longer keep citizens inside, as they are free to come and go through the gates. They therefore become boundaries rather than barriers. Boundaries are, by their very nature, moveable; barriers are designed to prevent entry and exit. Human beings flourish in a boundaried space but not in a barriered space. Boundaries can be crossed, explored, stretched and even broken down. Boundaries are essential for human and national identity and growth; barriers may help with human and national identity, but not with growth. In the New Jerusalem, there are boundaries but no barriers – the gates are open. This might seem strange since the Bible, time and again, shows great disdain for the area beyond the city gates. Generally the area outside the walls is regarded as the place where impure activities happen, where animals are killed before being sacrificed in the sanctuary, where the lepers walk, where criminals are stoned and where rubbish is dumped. The main pattern is that 'inside' is considered the established place of purity and order and 'outside' the place of impurity, danger and chaos.

To save Jerusalem from contamination the Jewish authorities therefore had Jesus crucified outside the city walls and buried there. But then, against every expectation, the resurrection and ascension, both pivotal events in the development of the Christian faith, happened outside the city walls. Salvation came from outside the walls. The place associated with rejection became the place of heavenly blessing. South American theologian Orlando Costas interprets this fact in stark terms when he states that 'Salvation lies outside the gates of cultural, ideological, political and socio-economic walls that surround our religious compound and shape the structures of Christendom' (Costas 1982: 191).

There is an intriguing story, recorded in 2 Kings 7.3–8, of four lepers to whom the gates of the city are locked. The city is besieged and near starvation, and so in desperation the four lepers risk all and venture into the camp of the enemy beyond the city wall. There they find the enemy has fled, leaving treasure and booty. They decide to share the news, and the treasure, with those inside the city and so become the agents of the city's liberation. Jesus, having been crucified beyond the safety of the city walls, likewise becomes the agent of the people's liberation. It is difficult for a well-defended society like today's to believe that its own liberation may come not from its centre, but from its marginalized communities. Similarly, the very shape of our industrialized cities is currently being turned inside out by the demise of industry and the revolutionary advent of post-modern, neo-liberal globalization. The old industrial activity – the great powerhouse of the British Empire, and until recently a centrepiece of our Western cities – has been sent to what was once so patronizingly called 'the Third World', whilst the old imperialist cultures are shocked to find that those from the margins are now in their midst.

As the peripheries become the centre and the centre moves to the 'edge city', will we recognize this as treasure and liberation?

Power and control

In the Christian economy, the Creator God is responsible not only for initiating creation but sustaining it. God does not abandon creation but shares ongoing responsibility for it. Whenever God's creatures make a mess, God is always there to redeem the mess. God has worked through the Hebrew patriarchs and prophets and most especially through his son Jesus Christ. And the Spirit of God continues to work through his disciples. Through worship, his followers are encouraged onwards and given energy to tread familiar and unfamiliar paths.

In the new urban areas we find repeatedly, however, that those who initiate and create these spaces have left the scene when questions of sustainability and cohesion hang in the balance.

As Chapter 4, 'Visionaries and Strategists', makes clear, any uniting 'vision' for the Thames Gateway has been changed, modified and even lost in its handling and management. In this respect government has abandoned its responsibility to the developers. An independent architect goes so far as to say that the Gateway, the largest regeneration area in Europe, has never had any overall plan or vision at all. Whether or not this is true, the fact that this is many people's perception is a serious indictment. With plans being passed from architects to strategists, to politicians, to investors and to developers, financial returns are given a higher priority than community development.

Lack of accountability is a serious problem. The elected government have abandoned power and control and given it over to unelected quangos and developers. There is a symbiotic relation between the well-being of a community and the role its members have in its governance and development. At present in the new urban areas, the rhetoric of power and the reality of where it is located are at variance with each other. The difficulty in determining just where the power does reside is leading to insecurity and anxiety at all levels of the Gateway and this needs to be addressed for the well-being of those living there, for deeply hidden authority is a dangerous commodity. In addition, determining just where power should reside calls for deep spiritual wisdom and sensitivity.

Feeding the soul in the new urban areas

It has already been made clear that, in order to grow and flourish, human beings need to feed the spiritual as much as the physical parts of their being. In this chapter, we have chosen to view people not as atomized individuals but as members of community. The African saying, 'I am because we are', succinctly expresses the fact that community is essential for human flourishing. This is contrary to the emphasis on individualism in Western culture. Today, the spiritual search is frequently regarded as an individual quest and if communities of like-minded people are met on the way, then all well and good, but if not, the quest continues anyway. Evidence of the spiritual search taking place outside communities of faith is apparent. The placing of flowers at the sites of road fatalities and other untimely deaths, the increase in marriages being conducted in hotels or other places of significance, and the scattering of cremated remains on a golf course or at a football stadium are indications of the human need to reach out and of spiritual searching. They are also indications that the Church is no longer meeting people at the significant points in their lives where people are most open to be met. It is the role of the Church to affirm the spiritual search while at the same time encouraging searchers to do this in community and in the context of worship of the Trinitarian God. The Church has a significant task on its hands as it discovers how it can best serve those outside its walls for the sake of God.

The commonness of this contemporary spiritual search has been viewed in a number of ways. It is an indication of people's continuing need to discover a sense of ultimate purpose and meaning in life. Some would view this as the Holy Spirit at work outside the walls of conventional religion, while others would see it as a reflection of individualist consumerism – the search to acquire personal spiritual fulfilment. Often spirituality is understood as more positive than religion. In the popular mind, spirituality is associated with wholeness and mystery whereas religion is associated with churches, ceremonies and, in a more negative way, with boredom and narrow-mindedness. But spirituality without religion can be like a boat without an anchor, blown around in undesirable directions. Religion, which is a structured system of beliefs and actions, can harness spiritual energy, making sure that it is used creatively, constructively and, where appropriate, in an orderly way. At its best, religion can make possible a fruitful dialogue with the past and prevent spirituality from repeating previous errors and being controlled and manipulated by a questionable minority. In addition, religion can, perhaps in a more concrete way than spirituality, underline the interrelatedness of humanity, thereby reinforcing the significance of the communal. A greater dialogue between religion and spirituality is required and it must be for the Church to facilitate that public dialogue.

So in conclusion, we ask, 'How is the soul being fed in new urban areas?' The book of Revelation lifted its readers to a vision which was wider and larger than their own limited perspectives in order to encourage and challenge them. What enables this broadening of perspective to happen in the new urban areas? Places of worship, where the soul as well as the body can be catered for, is one obvious need, but there have to be other places where people can rest and take account of what is going on within and around themselves. There should be public and communal art and artefacts which speak of life and energy and point to realities inside and outside of themselves and the world they inhabit. In his seminal book *The Geography of Nowhere*, James Howard Kunstler bemoans the effect of the culture of urban sprawl and the car on US society. Kunstler appeals for an investment in civic art, open and available to the ordinary pedestrian, in the search to reappropriate our humanity with a new vision for the common good (Kunstler 1993). Alastair

McIntosh, in his book *Soil and Soul: People versus Corporate Power*, writes, 'We need spaces where we can take rest, compose and compost our inner stuff, and become more deeply present to the aliveness of life' (McIntosh 2001: 280). Put theologically, in our new urban developments, where are the pointers towards transcendence? Put incarnationally, if we are confused and overwhelmed by the spiritual search, we can begin by feeding the hungry.

References

Costas, O., *Christ Outside the Gate*. Orbis, Maryknoll, NY, 1982.

Kunstler, J., *The Geography of Nowhere: The Rise and Decline of America's Man-Made Landscape*. Touchstone, New York, 1993.

McIntosh, A., *Soil and Soul: People versus Corporate Power*. Aurum Press, London, 2001.

Peterson, E., *Reverse Thunder: The Revelation of John and the Praying Imagination*. Harper and Row, San Francisco, 1988.

Radcliffe, T., *What is the Point of Being a Christian?* Burns and Oates, London, 2007.

Ward, G., *Cities of God*. Routledge, London, 2000.

8

Shaping the Church

We have now listened to residents, both new and old, from some of the communities in the Thames Gateway area; we have heard from planners, developers and those in the public sector about their perspectives on this particular set of developments. We have also looked at the wider picture of new urban areas and undertaken some basic typological thinking about the Church's praxis in this context. In this chapter, we return to the Thames Gateway communities we visited in Chapters 2 and 3 in order to observe the Church's response more critically and reflectively, and make some theological and strategic assessments of that response.

The snapshots we shall present here of church life across the Gateway show us a huge variety of responses as the Church shapes its Christian presence amongst these highly dynamic and complex new communities. Can we make any sense out of the diversity and confusion we have witnessed?

As we explored the new urban areas, and the older communities alongside them in the Thames Gateway, some common themes emerged. These were largely related to the changes in demography perceived by those living in these areas and are mainly about ethnicity, class, mobility and the extent to which residents wanted community locally or elsewhere.

A typology of religious affiliation in new urban areas

How do these large demographic forces such as ethnicity and mobility affect religious behaviour? For those who wish to meet together to worship within a common religious identity, we saw three major patterns of religious affiliation. First, there is religious affiliation associated with ethnic identity. Most of the big diasporic congregations based around African tribal or national identity are still located in London. For instance, the Kingsway

International Christian Centre (KICC) was founded in 1992 by Nigerian pastor Matthew Ashimolowo and has built up a membership of 12,000 on a 9.5-acre site. It has a strong cable TV presence, and educational, legal and counselling services, and it now offers services in French as well as English. The Glory House, founded by Pastor Dr Albert Odulele, has its main centre in Plaistow and bases its membership on strong family networks, commitment and evangelical crusades. However, there are a number of smaller churches dotted along the Gateway which are attracting worshippers from a broad area of other African nations and whose survival depends on the capacity to drive considerable distances to meet with 'your own', and sometimes even with extended family networks. This of course has been the case across London for many years and is not limited to African migrants: witness the existence of Asian Christian fellowships and the current debate in Roman Catholic circles as to how far Polish and other East European Catholic Christians need to integrate into the local parishes and how far separate language chaplaincies should exist.

Second, there are a small number of independent churches which could be broadly labelled 'charismatic' but which tend to describe themselves as community churches. The nature of their midweek fellowship is more likely to be based on e-mail or the Web, and utilizes mobile phone communication, drawing together like-minded sub-cells, social groups, or prayer groups on a network model. Again, they can attract members from a wide area and they see themselves as counter-cultural, 'gathered' churches working to a 'Bible-based' mission agenda.

Finally, there are the much more local churches, often mainstream institutional churches, usually with a membership within walking distance who see themselves as local churches for local people and frequently define their roles in terms of being a focus for neighbourhood needs and concerns, and in encouraging members to live out Christian values in their local society and beyond.

Rather than seeing these three patterns as distinct approaches to religious affiliation and underlying doctrinal commitment, we suspect they are better seen as lying on a continuous spectrum covering a range of models from 'associational' through to 'communal' – associational churches uniting those who gather or 'associate' around a common theme or identity, and 'communal' churches being more closely related to the local community in which the building or congregation is set. Also, the perspective of individual members may differ considerably from that of the leadership. We suspect that similar patterns may pertain within other major faith groups, although the associational element would of course predominate there, though we have only anecdotal evidence to support this claim.

There are many examples of each of these patterns of religious affiliation. If we start in South Newham, we immediately note in Canning Town (just north of the Thames Gateway redevelopment areas) the 'megachurches' of Glory House and Calvary Charismatic Baptist with combined memberships of several thousand. These churches are a major focus for Nigerian and Ghanaian Christians respectively. Both, however, also reach substantial populations of other ethnic groups, including increasingly large numbers of the white working-class host community – indeed, they now have programmes specifically designed to reach out in this way. Glory House in particular also has a big programme for local social action along with a clear evangelical preaching base.

Canning Town, Silvertown and North Woolwich, where we heard from both old and new occupants, present a very different picture. Smaller, churches of different nationalities, typically with 10 to 30 members, come and go, with few lasting more than five years. The two big Church of England Victorian 'barns' of St Luke and St Mark are both now in secular use. The first is a multi-storey internal structure with a wide range of community uses, including a doctor's surgery. The latter is the base for a Victorian-style music hall. The congregation of St Luke's has met in the local Church of England-aided school for the past 12 years, and has built up an impressive range of local projects based in other buildings around the parish. When it started meeting in the school its small but growing congregation began to attract new members who were unemployed or students, and its numbers rose from the teens to a regular Sunday congregation of 120. Now, however, they are experiencing a massive exodus out of the parish. On one recent Sunday five families told the vicar it was their last in Canning Town. Regeneration has pushed up local costs beyond the means of some, while others are seeking to better themselves by leaving the confines of the city. Numbers now fluctuate from 30 to 100, depending on weekend working patterns – many of those being folk who were unemployed ten years ago. Those who were students and now have qualifications also frequently join the flight further east along the Gateway.

Silvertown – now more frequently thought of as Britannia Village – covers a large part of the area. A nearby Baptist church was concerned that no Baptist presence was evident there and so began a fascinating church plant which has grown into a small local Baptist congregation meeting in the community hall and playing a significant part in trying to develop a strong sense of local community. St John's Anglican church – a 1960s building – hosts the local Roman Catholic congregation and an African church as well as the small, mainly African Church of England congregation. This particular congregation is seeing some of that African membership now moving to a new Pentecostal church which has opened by the Woolwich Ferry and which has a clear 'Bible-based' ministry, with a harsh judgement on the values of British society and a high expectation on committed members to engage, for example, in prayer ministry. Interestingly, the present vicar of the wider parish of St John's believes that the only way of reaching the new white middle class moving into what are frequently gated communities along the river is to reopen the old St Mark's church building as a local shrine to give newcomers a 'proper church' for weddings, funerals and baptisms, for which there is a growing demand. The present St John's building was conceived as a church and youth centre in the 1960s and the youth centre has been transformed over the last 40 years into a community centre, but it is increasingly cut off from the church worshipping area. Even the common physical entrance has now been replaced by separate doors. There is currently a project to help the church work with the youngsters who have been excluded from the church community centre! The priest concerned sees the work at this shared church centre as having an old 'mission church' feel, rather than being the established parish church to which parishioners might more naturally look. We make no judgements on that assessment, though we are aware that despite the belief of some that the traditional formularies of the Church have gone for ever, others will point to areas just a few miles away where the traditional pattern thrives.

Already then, we can see at the extreme western end of the Gateway different styles of the associational and communal behaviour we identified in our three models of religious affiliation. In Barking there is a not dissimilar picture in Thames View, the original council estate built in the 1950s. Here the Anglican church has a long-established centre which now houses the local Citizens' Advice Bureau, itself long supported by the Church Urban Fund and the local diocese. The evidence from the local population is that this is an accepted role for the Church of England church to perform. The parish also has the services of a Salvation Army captain who acts as industrial chaplain to the area and shares some of the worship leadership in the local church. Again, there is a Pentecostal church in one of the neighbouring warehouses, but little else in this vast area.

As we move further east again, out along the river to Purfleet, we find some of the most promising church experiments in the Essex Gateway. A small 'mission church' is now attached to Aveley parish, and when the present priest arrived in 2004 it housed a very small regular congregation of less than ten – in fact the records show that for several years three to six faithful souls kept a worshipping presence in what was felt to be a forgotten bit of working-class riverside. The present priest and his predecessor have both worked at being a strong personal presence in the locality and there is evidence in the responses from the wider community that they are recognized as significant. Both have worked as industrial chaplains to the range of industrial plants in the parish, and the present priest has also managed to attract local authority children's workers into the refurbished church building, so that it has become a neutral meeting-place for professionals serving this part of Thurrock, which has resulted in much more joined-up thinking across that sector. The congregation now numbers 15 to 25 a week, many of these only coming once a month and with a very wide range of nationalities reflecting the incomers.

Further east still at Little Thurrock, the Anglican congregation, swelled by Kenyan and other African Christians, has demolished its old ramshackle meeting hut and, along with the local health primary care trust, has built a large and impressive health centre and church where worship is exciting and holistic care is offered. The history of the Chafford Hundred development, built in the chalk quarry, has already been described in Chapter 3, where we spoke of the interesting way in which the need to develop community traditions has involved the church. The attempt to build a substantial shared worship centre has finally succeeded, but only after fraught inter-denominational negotiations. At present the free community church partner is meeting in a community centre elsewhere on the estate and looks unlikely to participate in what will end up being essentially a Church of England facility offering a substantial range of wider community provision.

Moving south across the river, the picture of church engagement with the wider community in Gravesend and around the new Ebbsfleet International Station is illustrated by the Old Town Hall Project being mounted by the local parish church of Holy Trinity, Dartford. This is an ancient church on the banks of the River Darent and is mentioned in the Domesday Book. It has had a social justice ethic for hundreds of years and has often worked with marginalized groups throughout its history. Ten years ago the church underwent a major renovation and is now a beautiful iconic building restored to its original beauty, with the additional benefits of a fully equipped hall, a purpose-built café and office space which houses health services and the Citizens Advice Bureau. The church continues to be firmly committed to community outreach, and various community development projects, such as advocacy work which has enabled a local estate to regain control of their community centre. This innovative management of a community estate was way ahead of the more recent asset-transfer programmes. The church-inspired management group now function under the inspiring name 'Faith in their Voices'. This group are people of faith, declaring their faith through public service. The project name indicates that the church has 'faith in the voices' of the local community and believes they can influence and change their own and their town's future. In developing its work, Holy Trinity church has built up an extensive network of trusted partners, which in turn has led to an interfaith project where the faith traditions in the Gravesend area can work together to promote the common good.

The Old Town Hall in Gravesend is a grand building that used to be the old courthouse, but was closed for some years. In its new incarnation, an innovative, imaginative and sizeable social enterprise project will be established, led by the local Church of the Holy Trinity, while a training scheme for those seeking to work in retail and IT will also be provided by the private sector. Statutory partners include Kent County Council and Gravesham Council, together with the probation and social services, who will be working with a variety of clienteles such as disaffected and underskilled youth and adults with learning difficulties. The voluntary and community sector will run art workshops and a community radio station, working with those excluded for their ethnicity or faith. This is a significant step toward making a beautiful old building, once a place of judgement, into a place of welcome for the whole community. The work of the new centre aims to bring about social cohesion and the inclusion of the most disadvantaged in the community, but is supported by those who are wealthier and can afford to frequent the new bistro and bar also located in the building. It attempts to address the needs of those who risk missing out on the opportunities presented by the Thames Gateway regeneration, by helping them to support and add value to it. One of the most important visions for this project is for the different constituents of the partnership to discover as they work together what spiritual renewal really means, and for this learning to permeate the community and contribute to community cohesion.

On the south side of the Thames, opposite Barking Reach, is the Thamesmead Estate, where an earlier and highly ambitious regeneration development was undertaken by the former Greater London Council in the 1960s. It is now earmarked to expand further under the Thames Gateway umbrella. Simon, the 'community priest', lives and works from his vicarage home with his family. He has been in post since 2005 and his ministry is parish-based, but without a church building. The developers of this estate did not see the need to provide a community space of any kind, so it consists of row upon row of housing, and little else. But the Church of England was keen at least to have a person based within this community to provide care and services for the incoming population. This post poses challenges and opportunities, both in terms of Simon's ministry and for the Church of England and the community. He describes it as an 'incarnational ministry – a ministry of presence – the communicative effect of living'. Simon is clear that it is of paramount importance for his presence in the community to be obvious, so he wears his clerical collar whenever he is out and about in order to make a statement about who and what he stands for. He maintains the usual links to schools and nursing homes and uses these networks to their fullest potential for extending his links into the community. Although he has no church building, he is part of the team ministry in Thamesmead, so this provides a Sunday church congregation for him, though few people from his own part of the parish would attend the main church, even though it is only two miles distant. He does find, however, that his locals do manage the distance for weddings or funerals. Planning regulations prevent him from gathering people for worship at the vicarage and there are no public halls – the school is not yet built – so Simon runs many alternative activities from his vicarage home as best he can. He and his wife run craft activities as an evangelistic tool, as a point of conversation to create relationships. There are also monthly discussion groups, Alpha courses and ladies' or men's evenings in the local pub. Simon describes his ministry as a 'ploughing ministry', in advance of the planting of any seeds. He feels he is at the very earliest stages of creating a Christian presence in a community made up of people who are new to the area, often new to the country and very new to the Christian faith.

This is a ministry of relationships, networks and personal service. The level of pastoral care Simon can give, he says, is significantly greater than that of other ministers because he has more time without a church building to run. He is enthusiastic about the opportunities for the future as he sets about working with the school, setting up a local shop ministry with a chat room in the hairdressers', and conducting a varied and engaging street ministry. However, he faces the challenge of maintaining his motivation when he has no team or group of Christian people immediately around him. Such groups as he does have are still very small and fragile and require intensive pastoral commitment. He misses the corporate aspect of church life. He is also unsure where he fits into the structures of his denomination, since he has no church council and no congregational membership – nor a regular church budget, since there is no income from congregational giving. These are issues that the wider church needs to address if this type of ministry is to be considered in other new and regenerating communities. However, Simon says he feels he is making a difference to people's lives, one person at a time, and his wider church denomination shares his view that it will take years for the ministry there to develop and consolidate. This is especially true as the development of the area is projected to take place in phases over the next ten years, so the dynamics and make-up of the community will be shifting constantly. We noticed in other areas of the Thames Gateway where other denominations had used this approach that they too found it a very labour-intensive investment which has yet to result in clearly viable congregations, although the work itself has value.

A diversity of church responses to the new urban areas: some emerging models

The consumer and prosperity gospel approach

We have noted a wide range of responses by churches to the new urban areas in and around the Thames Gateway. Our research and interviews have also indicated significant changes over the last 30 years in the way people think about themselves in relation to society. More people see themselves in society as consumers of products, services or leisure activities and some churches have responded by accepting that mindset, some even pandering to it. For example, some offer worshippers a self-fulfilling sense of God in which God is expected to grant their stated petitions – some of the new churches actually promising guaranteed answers to prayer. We have also observed a retreat by some into the religion of simplistic certainty – based on straightforward, often literal understandings of the Bible.

The institution

Other incomers view themselves and their relationship with the wider society and with God altogether differently, and what happens when people create a new community with such a range of self-understandings is therefore complex. If a church already has an institutional presence, however small, with its own building, then, we have observed, it may quickly become the focus for migrants from other congregations. The history of Harlow New Town is salutary. It was built on the extant medieval villages, but the Church of England nevertheless decided to build, in addition to a new town-centre church, several new neighbourhood churches and attempted to close the medieval buildings, which they felt were in the wrong place. One church was even converted into a museum. Two others were treated as daughter churches scheduled for closure as soon as possible. However, they have paradoxically thrived as the new modern centres of worship have struggled. Is it an accident that through the 1970s to the 1990s the strongest church memberships proved to be in the old buildings? Interestingly, the first priest to serve in Chafford Hundred noted that parents wanted to have their children baptized in the 'pretty old church' across the main road – in a completely different parish – almost as though it were another world untouched by the messiness of their new estate. It may simply be that the old building was easily recognizable, but it may also have been that a religious site was being thought of as escape, which makes it doubly difficult for the church to raise its prophetic voice.

Pete Ward, in his book *Liquid Church* (Ward 2002), warns against the tendency of churches in situations of rapid change to revert to nostalgic models of religion and to our heritage sites, which, although moribund, are not necessarily numerically or financially weak. Anglican priest and theologian Rod Garner, quoting J. Williams, writes,

> The local church . . . might abandon its sacred buildings . . . setting up house fellowships, opening an office or shop front in the high street with professional staff on hand to deal with a range of religious and social needs, and working in close cooperation with social services, medical practices and schools . . . All this would be meant to equip the church to respond to the secular sphere rather than acting as a sanctuary set over against it.　　　(Garner 2004: 128)

We cannot talk about the incarnational Church – the Church engaged in a physical way in the midst of a community – without considering the place of church buildings, but this presents us with a dilemma. A church building can be a fine icon of the presence of God in its community. On entering, a sense of the numinous presence of the Divine may be quite tangible, prompting a deeper openness to God and an awareness of the immanence of the transcendent. In such surroundings a congregation may become energized spiritually to work for the values of the Kingdom of God in that community. In new urban areas a church building may well be the only public space. What operates inside it and flows from it could prove crucial to the new and diverse residents. Where the development includes heavily gated apartment blocks, isolating their residents, the Church speaks to that sense of isolation by offering as an alternative a place of community and relationship and by pointing to the ultimate purpose of life.

In the 1970s and 1980s bodies like the Tavistock Institute for Human Relations and the Grubb Institute noted that the finding of dependable objects beyond the self is absolutely essential for the health of all human societies. For the religious believer the ultimately dependable 'object' is God. The need for times and places where one can retreat safely in order to gain the strength to engage again with life in community may relate closely to the human need for the church building – the local shrine. Perhaps we need to revisit these studies if we are to make the best use of our church buildings and not treat them simply as problems. A 'church which looks like a church' may prove a great gift, whose value in the hearts and minds of those amongst whom it is set must be rediscovered before we discard it. When deciding whether a church should be built and in what style, we not only have to look seriously at the context of the geographical area – how it is being developed and by whom – we also need a thorough understanding of the diverse and complex range of people who live in the locality and how they might see and enter the building. We must have a passion for our faith and for the community in which we are set – and our buildings should be icons of those passions.

The holistic paradigm

Unfortunately, the statistics for church attendance nationally in the UK, whatever the blips of 'recovery' or 'new interest in spirituality' may occasionally promise, show long-term decline over more than a century. Bob Jackson, in his book *Hope for the Church*, paints a scary picture of children's Sunday attendance decreasing from 2.4 million in 1910 to 1.8 million in 1930, down to 250,000 in 1980 – and, he adds, the decline is continuing (Jackson 2002: 97). Yet the desire for some kind of religious dimension to life, be it a search for meaning, 'spirituality' or whatever, seems deeply rooted in the human psyche. We found a substantial amount of evidence for this, not least in the search for fitness and a new, perfected identity. For example, we were struck by this account from a regular gym user, who is also a member of a local church:

The gym that I attend each week is on a new urban development just inside the Gateway, near Greenwich. It is not a wealthy area, in fact the opposite. It has a lot of atrocious social housing that is currently being completely demolished and the residents decanted to make way for a massive new development to take place over the next ten years, which will include mixed housing tenure, job opportunities and speedy transport links into London. No matter what time of day or night I attend, even up to 11 p.m., there are always people in there working out, relaxing or taking classes. It is a high-quality health and leisure centre, hosting a Costa café, restaurant, plasma screens as well as the high-tech gymnasium with Jacuzzi and steam rooms, etc. At first glance this seems strange. One is prompted to ask, 'Who is this gym for?' The locality is about to be emptied of residents, yet the foresight and planning of the leisure industry is ahead of us in the Church and not only are they catering for the current clientele who elect to travel to the gym, with its massive car park for 200, but also for the new community who will be coming in and who choose to buy the leisure and health components of life.

Andy Barclay-Watt, a Christian leader in Manchester, says,

> A lot of people going to clubs don't feel satisfied with their lives; so they'll try to improve how they look and feel. But there are some significant deep-rooted issues which we can help people face at the same time ... The industry recognizes that people want 'wholeness' and 'well-being'. Those are big buzz words. It's about mind and spirit, as well as body. (quoted in Draper 2006)

In 2004 an article appeared in the *Guardian* in which Brocas Burrows, manager of an upmarket London-based health club called Third Space, explains the philosophy behind the club's name: 'The philosophy is that you have three spaces in your life – home, work and here ... It's the third most important space in our members' lives – and for some of them it's even higher. It's a spiritual centre in a way' (Jeffries 2004). Similarly, the success of New Age shops and therapies should cause us to reflect on how many people use these to acknowledge the sacredness of things around them, the interconnectedness of all God's creation and the need for concern about our environment. Meanwhile, health clubs which have hosted Alpha courses have reported that people who attend say they would never have participated if the course had been held on church premises, but as it was held in their club they felt they could 'give it a go'. This speaks loudly to those of us working in new urban areas, where community life is vulnerable to atomization. Can we, or should we, learn from the pre-packaged gym methodology of evangelism, which seeks to provide a holistic service to their consumers based on the criteria of customer uniqueness and market choice?

The chaplaincy model

Another model of engagement we have observed across the Thames Gateway is the chaplaincy model – the critical friend present alongside people as they meet together in various areas of society. Chaplaincy in schools and hospitals, of course, has a long and valued history, and industrial chaplaincy formed much of the cutting edge of Christian engagement and theological reflection in post-war Britain. Fascinatingly, in the Thames Gateway, chaplaincy to the retail consumer malls of Lakeside and Bluewater has grown as traditional local industry has declined. In Chelmsford, just outside the Gateway, the Marconi electronics factory has recently imploded, shrinking from 5,000 workers to just a few hundred, whilst simultaneously the Lakeside retail centre has grown to employ 5,000, and even more at the busy Christmas season. Interdenominational chaplaincy has grown with it. And the Gateway is seeing this kind of Christian presence spreading elsewhere, with chaplaincies not simply to shops and offices but to the police service and other significant institutions across the area.

A place to belong

The local church is well placed to offer a sense of belonging to those suffering the isolation and atomization resulting from suburban sprawl and lack of community amenities. What community facilities exist are often too expensive or too remote for the poorer members in the community, geared as they are to the market-place rather than the inclusion of all. The church may therefore be the only place where everyone can gain entry. One vicar refers to his small building on a new estate as a 'hostel for the homeless', in that so many local residents have no sense of belonging to their new locality as it seems to lack an obvious identity. The church can become a symbol of a new or emerging identity and if it flourishes, it can put 'soul' into a barren landscape. It can do this by spotting the story of the community emerging within the locality and celebrating it. Many of the newly built estates and towns of the past were built to accommodate people who already had a common heritage – perhaps having left a demolished inner-city area – but, as we have constantly acknowledged, we now live in such a globalized society that, as people pour into our newly built urban settlements, they bring a wide variety of cultures with them.

However, it is important to realize that within the Thames Gateway the newcomers often hail from cultures that have strong Christian roots and we must not be slow to capitalize on that great gift. Religious groups are often the first to organize themselves in new areas and in that process they will usually look for a building to call 'home'. Religion is a communal affair, not a privatized spirituality, and so requires physical place to be at its best. Within these religious places, iconic symbols will be needed to give the religious community a physical cutting edge and make the worshippers feel at home. Bland 'sacred space' pleases no one because it fails to recognize the physical nature of religion, but planners and developers do not usually realize this and offer only barren empty space for religious groups to meet. We have much work to do if our new urban areas are to include places which feed the locality's soul.

Other strategic responses to new urban areas

Throughout this exploration into our new urban areas, a large number of crucial ethical issues have repeatedly arisen. We have learnt of cohesive communities being broken apart by the intrusion of new developments, listened to anecdotal evidence of the emergence of 'new town blues', the rise in mental illness as community breaks down, the doleful lack of facilities amidst suburban sprawl, the commodification of life as a consequence of the over-mighty market, and the poor construction quality of some of the new developments. These, and so much more, are a threat to human flourishing, and where such ethical concerns are evident, there the Church must be.

The Church at local and national level has a gospel duty to engage with these issues – to be alongside those who suffer as a consequence, and to work to bring wisdom and justice to bear on the regeneration decisions that affect the lives of so many. The Church has a great deal of experience, built up over many generations, of working to create trust and mutual care within communities. However, it sometimes feels as though we have little experience to go on when building community from scratch in the new urban areas. We do have examples of ongoing ecumenical work in the New Towns but even these have not always flourished. We will therefore do well to engage with urbanologists, radical geographers, planners and developers, so that we can be well informed to meet the challenge. There are examples across the Thames Gateway where this engagement is already happening, as local congregations and clergy forthrightly participate in negotiation and discussion with the decision-makers. Many have taken on the responsibility of membership of local strategic partnerships, regional offices, development delivery vehicles and the like. In Basildon, the parish church council meet regularly with town planners, developers and strategists in order to bring the human perspective to a major regeneration programme for the town centre. In Southend, a parish priest has become a director of the urban regeneration company Renaissance Southend, because, he says, he felt a clear call from God to get involved rather than just let things happen around him and his parishioners. In East London a number of local church leaders have been elected to local government office. They seek to offer, on behalf of the Church, an alternative ethic which does not put money before people but sees communities as the seedbed of human flourishing – seeking to put soul back into community.

In Chelmsford diocese, Bishop Laurie Green has been appointed as Lead Bishop on Regeneration and Community Development in order to maintain a high profile on the issues surrounding the new areas, and he has encouraged the development of ecumenical study and action groups in each of the regeneration locales within Essex and East London. Canon Duncan Green has been appointed by the churches to coordinate the Christian voice regarding the negotiations about the heritage benefits that should accrue to East London from the Olympics site in Stratford. At national level, Bishop Stephen Lowe speaks for the Church of England on these issues, and the Church has set aside £7.2 million as the first tranche of investment in projects in the new urban areas for the next three years, with research and development very much to the fore. At local parish level resources are becoming available, not least through the

Web, for those who wish to engage with the ethical, social, political and environmental implications. This is the new shape of the Church as it seeks to address the new shape of our urban scene.

But when local Christians take up the challenge they often feel as if they have strayed into foreign territory. They encounter planners, developers and government sector workers whose vocabulary and systems of working seem altogether alien. We the Church have to learn to work with new agendas, and to work to mutually agreed targets with efficiency and professionalism. We enter a new world of LAAs, LSPs, 106 Agreements, but as soon as we have mastered these mysterious acronyms, then they are replaced by others. We learn to work to imposed time constraints that run counter to our church culture, and continually have to guard against losing our Christian agenda when partnering the professional players in the regeneration game. Some Christian groups regret that now they have sealed a deal for funding, they must submit to the agendas of their paymasters. Others have happier experiences and delight in working alongside those who bring new gifts from other agencies and disciplines.

Not only do we, the churches, have difficulty engaging with the world of regeneration, but we also find a frightening degree of religious illiteracy amongst those who would engage with us in return. They often despair at the inability of the faiths to speak with one voice during negotiations, or at the unaccountability of faith leaders to their constituencies. On the other hand, some are thoroughly surprised that at times the denominations and faiths will put up a strongly united front on some issues. The East of England Churches Network, through its Faiths Council, has offered instructive seminars for leaders of churches and other faiths to meet and learn alongside practitioners from the private and public sector in order to find where the synergy lies beneath all these conflicting vocabularies and expectations. Other organizations are following suit, and in doing so soon realize that many of the planners and developers are themselves people of faith who struggle to hold the two worlds of faith and regeneration together in their own lives. As we meet together and learn from one another, the most important challenge of all is to reach across the divides of ethos and culture enough to understand and care for one another for the long term, rather than contenting ourselves merely with understanding each another only long enough to close a deal.

Conclusion

The New Testament word for church is *ekklesia*, the calling out and gathering of people with a special purpose. This could also serve as a definition for new and emerging urban communities if the Holy Spirit is allowed in. Church is about being the Body of Christ, so it should provide a spiritual landscape in which we can encounter the Divine through worship and sacrament. This in turn should prove so restorative and transformative that it leads us back out towards community encounter. In other words, what happens in church must take us to a place outside of it.

The church has an important job to do. It needs to consider its models of ministry and ask itself some important questions. Is it going to be a market-shaped church, trendy, changing all the time to keep up with the latest technology and ideas? We must remember that, while the market often transcends boundaries, it can do this so insistently that, ultimately, anything goes. Will the Church follow a community model, seeking to draw in, include and empower local people? Will it consider the selective model, where people can pick and choose a church regardless of geographical location? We have encountered examples of all these types of church in the Gateway, each model having theological and social consequences – not least to do with their own understanding of their purpose. We should be careful about how and why we reshape ourselves, for whilst we must strive for 'accessibility', that motivation can easily be lost in the quest for 'acceptability', with all its attendant dangers to the integrity of the faith.

But, most important of all, the Church in the new urban area is there to celebrate, in worship and in its daily life, the very presence of the transcendent God in our midst. The presence of the immanent Holy One will oblige the congregation to engage with the ethical issues, but the invitation must go out to the whole locality to join in the celebration of the Good News, for the Church must be the first to proclaim that, in our new urban areas, there is also something to sing about!

Building Utopia?

References

Draper, B., 'Change of Tune at the Gym: Let's Get Spiritual'. *Church Times*, 7494 (27 October 2006).

Garner, J., *Facing the City*. Epworth Press, Peterborough, 2004.

Jackson, B., *Hope for the Church: Contemporary Strategies for Growth*. Church House Publishing, London, 2002.

Jeffries, S., 'The Tyranny of the Gym'. *Guardian*, 5 January 2004.

Ward, P., *Liquid Church*. Paternoster, Carlisle, 2002.

148

9

Urban visions and urban values

At the end of Chapter 1 we outlined some of the history of the development of post-suburban areas, and speculated as to some of the human development and theological issues these rapidly emerging settlements might raise. Having mapped the terrain of these new urban areas in Chapters 1–5 and reflected in Chapter 6 on the complexity and diversity of experiences and issues in this terrain, we outlined in Chapters 7 and 8 what we consider to be some of the key theological and ecclesiological principles. We believe that these principles (and the praxis that embodies them) not only shed light on new urban areas such as the Thames Gateway, but have wider resonances for and applications to the mission and ministry of the Church as a whole.

We concluded Chapter 1 by raising what we considered a fundamental question regarding these new urban areas: whether they might 'offer future generations sustainable and delightful places to live, where human beings can flourish in every way, or if these British versions of the edge city are taking us to the brink of a social and spatial precipice'. We now seek to answer this question, taking into account the many perspectives gathered on our journey through the Thames Gateway, but also, in the spirit of the *Faith in the City* and *Faithful Cities* reports, to ask the key question lying behind all urban theology; namely, 'What makes a good city – what makes a flourishing and sustainable built environment?'

We undertake this assessment by using, for one final time, the conceptual framework of Utopias and dystopias. In the first part of this chapter, we reflect on the more dystopic aspects of the new urban areas. In the second part, we reflect on those aspects of these areas and church engagement within them that begin to put further flesh on the bones of our more Utopian and visionary understanding of what makes a good city.

Dystopia: the reality of the imperfect city

Throughout these chapters, our search for the fulfilment of the Utopian promise of the new urban areas has issued in very mixed, if not disappointing, results. Those older residents who have encountered new developments in their communities have often felt ignored by planners, encroached upon by builders' equipment and marginalized by the incomers. They have often voiced their concern that their old community has been ripped apart and that the new 'is not for the likes of us'. Incomers have sometimes welcomed a new start and the possibility of new opportunities but have soon bemoaned the lack of promised local amenities and have sensed a new isolation. On the other hand, many have said that they are benefiting from the investments they have made and the ease of access to the office, the shopping mall and leisure facilities – even though these all come at a price. Many feel a buzz on looking at the iconic buildings and enjoy the diversity of the mobile and cosmopolitan lifestyle for which the new areas cater. Planners and developers have their own take on each new development, the more outspoken raising serious questions about construction quality, site location and backroom political dealing. Those whose task it is to care for residents in these new urban areas complain that the infrastructure is lacking, and the old mindsets of local authorities and the new target-driven bureaucracy are limiting the delivery of care. In Bangalore, young executives throwing themselves from top-storey windows, and in the Thames Gateway the incidence of mental illness, both point to a malaise at the heart of the lifestyle for which the new buildings are designed.

The idolatrous dream

The new urban buildings we encountered in the Gateway seem on the face of it to be reinforcing the values of the global economic and political hegemony – the sacralizing of the market-place, where competition reigns at the expense of cooperation – and this divides already fragmented groups rather than inculcating a strong sense of belonging and community. This political and economic mindset of market-place competition is often referred to as 'neo-liberalism' and our use of the term throughout this chapter is strongly influenced by the work of Doreen Massey (2007). Unless this neo-liberal ideology is a touchstone, the present developments symbolic of this mindset are simply uninspiring. It is as if the boastful consumption of post-modern global neo-capitalism comes face to face with the needs of the planet in the 'wow-factor' towers (to quote John Prescott's famous term) and the urban sprawl which constitute so much of our new urban areas. We can see this in the way that present development acquires land essentially as something to be exploited for profit rather than as potentially sacred space where human beings may grow together and flourish. The rhetoric of the developer's sales pitch often promises the latter but, as we saw in Chapter 4 from interviews with, for example, our housing-group executive, the resulting reality is more clearly the former. When God promises the elect a land flowing with milk and honey, we can either interpret that as the guarantee of human fulfilment and commonwealth, or the chance to sell the milk and honey and buy the admiration of the less entrepreneurial masses. The neo-liberal mindset is more subtle than this, obviously, but it is certainly all-embracing. As A. P. Davey insightfully states,

> Cities are remodelled to make them spaces in which the key activities of neo-liberalism can flourish with the least resistance. The cities of Europe and North America become command centres based on service industries, consumption and culture. The cities of the global south vie for regional dominance as points in the command chain. Manufacturing moves easily as cheaper locations emerge . . . – those unable to compete find themselves on the periphery, those who succeed are drawn to the centre. Neither motion can be traced in the terms of locational geography, but rather such positioning becomes apparent through the renewal of a city's infrastructure, or through the access of its citizens to key resources within the global economy.
>
> (Davey 2008: 36)

Davey here helpfully points to how neo-liberal relationships are redefining place, and organizing hierarchies of power which impinge directly upon our daily lives in the new urban areas.

Creativity is one of God's greatest gifts and we see it abundantly in the planning, designing and building of our new urban developments. But whenever human beings become creative we also have to guard against the sin of idolatry – sacralizing our own inventions and inventiveness. If we worship our own constructions – be they mindsets, cultures or structures – we allow them to rule over us and they begin to make the world in their own image. Globalization and market neo-liberalism have been allowed to assume imperialistic powers and our new urban areas are in danger of becoming nothing but colonies. In this regard it is interesting to see our own British government now pressuring its UK regions to adopt a more economy-driven approach to regeneration, stripping out the Regional Assemblies and trimming budgets on the softer edge of community investment. This is very much the same mindset.

Some developments are simply modest variations on the old style of house-building and town development, but most are deeply indebted to the new global forces at work, though unfortunately, this is not always easy to see. It is interesting to note how the government and developers answer the concerns of conservationists that building X per cent of the newly planned housing on flood plains may not only be dangerous for the future of those who live in those houses but may also prevent the drainage of surplus water from surrounding areas. Whilst developers direct us to look at the high standard to which those houses will be built, government ministers are heard on radio and TV saying that in order to make a high percentage of the new homes 'affordable' it is absolutely essential to build on flood plains – a clear admission that the houses will be of a lower standard in those areas. If this is not neo-liberalism exploiting the cash value of land, what is it?

In making an idol of market profit we are hiding reality from ourselves, thinking that somehow the market can be relied upon to save us from ourselves. The Hebrew prophets constantly had to warn the city that serving other gods would bring destruction (see, for example, Jeremiah 15.18) – just as Jesus reminded the devil that it was a great temptation to rely on anything but 'every word that comes from the mouth of God' (Matthew 4.4). King Canute, who once ruled vast areas of the Thames Gateway, could only convince his courtiers that they must 'get real' by proving that their false hope in his abilities to save his lands was illusory. He had no power to prevent nature from being nature. The brash promises of the 'iconic' buildings of neo-liberal globalization actually hide the truth that all empires eventually have to give way to those they oppress. An icon, after all, is a picture on a screen or in a chapel which, if touched upon, open us up to a whole new world that lies beyond and through it. The iconic building may have a 'wow factor', but the single mum pushing her pram past it on a Monday morning will probably see that behind the icon is a world not to be trusted. As we have already implied in Chapters 1 and 7, that world offers a 'city of endless desire' (Ward 2000) which will not in the end fulfil one's deepest needs.

The ultimate irony is that whilst exposing the planet to such risk, the market of global neo-liberalism promises security. Time and again, we have observed, shopping malls have been designed specifically to cocoon shoppers and assure them that all is well. Heavily patrolled by security staff, these air-conditioned, well-lit, aspiring spaces give every impression that it is in the market that human beings will find both contentment and fulfilment. Our visits to Milton Keynes, Lakeside and Bluewater all offered the same risk-averse environment, as if to say, 'Your investment in this mind-set gives you the security you need, and a return at no risk. All that you want is here and we hold your status as "shopper" in the highest regard.' What more could one want? And yet the real evidence throughout the world is that the global market-place is highly volatile and fickle. Finance can flood in one minute, but can just as easily take its winnings and go elsewhere – after all, it has the whole world to choose from. What we have learnt to call 'global flows' bring capital and populations to honey-pots around the world and at the touch of a button begin to remove them. Today's prophets warn us, just like the Hebrew prophets of old, that to put our trust in the 'chariots of Egypt', or in any other imperial global power-base, is to court disaster.

Some non-biblical perspectives can also shed light on the propensity to idolatry highlighted by the dynamics of the globalized economy as it impinges on new urban areas such as the Thames Gateway. Crucial to this perspective is, first, how the existing landscape (including both human community and non-human environment) is viewed and, second, what it might mean to be 'in relationship' – to be 'rooted' in one's community and culture.

It was the influential anthropologist Clifford Geertz who, following Weber, identified the importance of a local language made up of distinctive words, gestures and artefacts. These are evolved from a negotiation of dense and overlapping metaphors, a 'field' of

153

tales, histories and meanings that help identify the life, worldview and even the type of god that is significant to and distinctive of that local community. Geertz referred to this complex matrix of meanings and interpretations as a 'web of significance' which local communities and individuals weave for themselves. What has emerged powerfully from the various stories and patterns of behaviour in Chapters 2 and 3 is the ongoing importance of these personal and community narratives – particularly for those existing communities whose identity is being radically challenged by new housing and new residents who have very different priorities and worldviews.

We also saw the importance of these webs of significance reflected in the views of immigrants of long standing who kept alive (often through churchgoing) a sense of those values, ways of communicating and spiritualities they had brought with them from their native African context. On the surface, everything that has emerged in this book regarding the economic, planning and cultural priorities of the Thames Gateway points away from this idea of a richly textured local landscape – one that signifies your identity and purpose in life. What we appear to have instead is a series of exurban landscapes built for mobility and convenience around transport and retail hubs with a homogeneous design brief, largely dislocated from the local cultural and topographical landscape. These new areas are built quickly and cheaply to appeal to the idea of high turnover and mobility – not cultural continuity and long-term stability. Indeed, there is anecdotal evidence to suggest that buildings constructed as recently as five years ago are already showing signs of stress and decay.

One of the more memorable indictments of the Thames Gateway planning and development process in Chapter 4 came from the architectural adviser: 'One major question we are concerned about is the identity of the new community. If we excavate an ancient city we will come across some physical structures around which the community was organized. Religious and social institutions and establishments always played a major role. But these new plans do not have these as priorities' (p. 62).

This idea of 'excavating roots' reminds us of the real purpose of the land and the human social interaction it should foster. It is not there just for profit and exploitation but as a gift from God – as a locus for human flourishing and for the good of all species.

Preserving the idolatrous dream: the idolatry of risk management

The dominant tone of the Thames Gateway discourse is, on the other hand, more concerned with managing risk to personal and corporate investment in property and land than seeing the land as a gift from God. These financial investments seem to have a disproportionate effect on the way people see their relationship to their environment. Thus we noted in Chapter 2 the pressure amongst some of our existing residents to sell their housing in order to capitalize on the demand generated by proximity to new transport, retail or investment hubs – to take the money and settle down in the countryside or abroad. Those who had recently moved into the new areas of housing, particularly those closest to the London end of the Gateway, declared themselves very proud of the 'excellent investment returns' for the past three years or so. We also heard from new residents in Waterstone Park, south of the Dartford Bridge, that most people like themselves have bought a new house in the Kent suburbs 'either as a temporary expedient or as an investment'.

Some new house-owners in Chapter 3 referred to the existing social housing in their areas as an 'eyesore', which, if improved, would 'see property prices rising significantly'. Elsewhere in our early chapters there are several references to the fear of crime and especially lack of discipline amongst young people, and to the need for a sense of personal or family security. This has created a palpable perception of the need to exert control over one's environment, as reflected in a growing sense of retreat into the safe, private and defended space of the home or gated environment. It has also been a significant theme in our interviews and reflections that some of this need for private and defended space is clearly driven by wariness or even fear of the high levels of ethnic and cultural diversity to be found in these new settlements. Some new residents appear quite comfortable with close neighbours of different background and ethnicity – others, however, are clearly not. Ideally the rich mix of ethnic and cultural communities choosing to live in the Thames Gateway would be the source of a vibrant and diverse civil society. However, this prevalent wariness of otherness might well prevent this.

The paradox of this illusory desire for absolute safety, control and predictability in an otherwise rapidly changing and perhaps atomizing world is exposed when one also considers the environmental challenges affecting the Thames Gateway region. If predicted trends in global warming are in any way accurate, then rising global sea levels, plus ever more erratic but ever higher amounts of rainfall, will undermine all attempts at micro-management of risk. Much housing already exists on flood plains, and in order for projected housing targets to be met, much more new housing will have to be built on them. Our interviews indicate a general denial of the potential catastrophic threat from flooding and the potential inadequacy of the flood defence systems currently in place.

Risk, community and identity

As we reflected in Chapter 7, the Christian faith is centred upon relationships – the perfect relationship within the essence of our God as Father, Son and Holy Spirit, which in turn is offered to us in Jesus' invitation to his followers to be in him as he is in the Father (John 17.23). Our identity as Christians is therefore to be found in community – as the African proverb already quoted in Chapter 7 has it, 'I am because we are.' Groups tend to define themselves in terms of their boundaries separating them from others, but the Christian knows that since the manner of the Holy Spirit is to 'blow where it chooses' (John 3.8) and to transcend barriers, so the Christian shares with some of the other world faiths a holistic vision of reality. There is a radical interrelatedness at the heart of reality, so as Leonardo Boff affirms, 'Ecology constitutes a complex set of relationships. It includes everything, neglects nothing, values everything, is linked together. Based on this we can recover Christianity's most early perception: its conception of God' (Boff 1993: 115). This is the truth with which 'globalization' conjures, seeking to acknowledge and embody the radical interrelatedness of the globe and of all people via networks of shared trade, investment and knowledge.

However, the neo-liberal ideological aspects of globalization misunderstand the proper nature of that relationship. Christianity proclaims that that relationship is one of deferential love, the world thus mirroring the self-giving love which is the inner heart of the Holy Trinity. This is why the creation and nurturing of community is of such importance to Christians as they seek to live out the Kingdom of God on earth as it is in heaven. But how can this be done under the apparently powerful global hegemony of the neo-liberal market's commodification of land?

We might look for comfort at a city like Naples which, unlike some western homogenized cities, seems to work so naturally with its environment and ecology. It does not deny the realities of suffering – it is not sterile and risk-resistant – but grows and contracts organically rather than being set upon by outsiders who would impose their will upon its style and culture. In the UK, contemporary civic identity is far too often simply a new brand invented for a city or town by regeneration consultants seeking to sell the place to external investors. Only those towns and cities with the most strongly rooted cultures can withstand the pressure to conform to one-size-fits-all office towers and high-street branding.

Within this ideological environment many people of goodwill look for ways to help society benefit from the best aspects of the market-place whilst guarding against its worst excesses. They know that suburban sprawl and the resulting gridlocked infrastructure must eventually seize up, and seek alternatives. Many argue for population density as against sprawl, but then find it extremely difficult to attract house buyers to invest in such a heavily urbanized lifestyle – they 'want sustainability as long as I can live where I like'. And since individual choice is the mantra of neo-liberalism, the rich can vote with their pocketbooks against sustainable living. Similarly, if there is a market for single-person homes then the developers will fulfil it, even if it reinforces the break-up of family life and the uneconomical use of resources. Some opt for moving in alongside older urban communities only to find that others do the same, ratchet up land values, gentrify the area and price out the original occupants.

Gentrification gives the impression that an area has been regenerated, but this is at the expense of the poor, who simply have to move downmarket. To offset the fear of the urban, many incomers live in gated communities and seek some sort of neighbourliness there. But to define a community in terms of such separation and fear is not creating community as the Christian understands it. The difficulty is that a space only becomes a treasured place when it has a history, a story, that tells people about where it has come from, a present sense of itself and what it stands for, and a future which can be owned. However, in today's new urban areas, the 'space of flows' obliterates the stories of the past and offers a present culture which is rarely different from so many other places. As we saw in Chapter 8, some groups, including the Church, can offer a tribal sameness to which people can cling, but we are searching for an identity which, like the Holy Spirit, offers a freedom to be and the challenge to become.

As we look together to the future – the Christian's lodestone for the present – so we note also the current obsession with the heritage of the past. The Chinese say that unless we know where we have been, it will be impossible to map where we want to go – but many of the new urban areas manifest not a true listening to the story of the extant community but what we might call the 'Disneyfication' of the local culture. Again, it is as if the continuity of ecology and of community is no longer perceived, just as the digital watch no longer offers us an analogue hand sweeping round the hours, connecting one time to the next, but the pulsing of digits; not a cognizance of history, but simply points in time. Much of the newly built environment will be what is comically called 'Martini' housing, harking back to the advertisement which proclaimed 'any time, any place, any where', always the same. Local culture, history and form is forgotten since so many houses are built on a sectional framework, so that an architect has no chance to build in distinctive features to celebrate the uniqueness of place. So the people who live in these homes will spend hours on the Internet researching their family trees, or they will go to interactive heritage museums and walk the canals in order to touch something of the identity they crave. The older church buildings lend a hand to this in a way that modern office-like churches never can.

Utopia: the search for the good city

We believe that Christians can offer the outline of an urban future that is worth envisioning. In our estimation, such an outline would be one which, in a powerful metaphor we have already considered in this chapter, would carefully examine the nourishing roots of its own identity while confidently envisioning a flourishing future. Before spelling that out in more detail, we pause to consider the urban vision that others have offered – three key principles for the good city which we within the church community can reflect upon and allow to shape our own performative engagement in new urban areas.

Sustainable communities of well-being

The UK government, in its report *Sustainable Communities* (ODPM 2003), dreamt of friendly places that are prosperous, safe and clean, with open spaces and facilities accessible to all who need them. In addition they felt that inclusivity, environmental sensitivity, good design and construction, fair distribution and connectivity were important factors. The New Economics Foundation speaks of happier communities with education for well-rounded people, physical, emotional, mental and social well-being, and the encouragement of a strong civil society and active citizenship (Shah and Marks 2004). Leone Sandercock, an Australian community planner, writes in her study *Cosmopolis II: Mongrel Cities*,

> I dream of a city in which action grows out of knowledge and understanding; where *you* haven't got it made until you can help others to get where you are or beyond . . . where no one flaunts their authority and no one is without authority . . . where community values and rewards those who are different . . . where 'community' is caring and sharing responsibility for the physical and spiritual condition of the common living space . . . I want a city that is run differently than an accounting firm.   (Sandercock 2003: 219)

Such imaginative and exciting visions make it clear that we are certainly not alone in striving for an alternative understanding of how urban spaces should function. The human imagination at its best is inspired with a vision of community which is not confined to the worst excesses of the globalized market model. It is as if deep in the heart of the human spirit it is mysteriously known that we are made in the image of a Trinitarian God who stands against the prevailing ideology and summons us to a new creation – the New Jerusalem.

Contested public spaces

The Church should join these other people of goodwill and those groups and institutes who are on this same journey – the great project of envisioning urban community and treasured place, indeed becoming one of those places where this process can unfold. Public theology in the market-place of ideas, rather than consumer goods in the market-place of enthralment, could then help people enjoy the contested space of the city. This will be a learning process – like the journey of the prodigal son, who had to venture out into a muddled and tempting world before valuing the community of his homeland and the generosity of his father. This communal process of discovery will be a multidisciplinary journey, travelling with artists, radical geographers of space, urbanologists and planners, and most especially, those who are now seeking God in the new urban areas. It will be a journey to discover new understandings of both place and time – place for who we are and where we belong, and time for community commitment, rhythm and locatable relationships.

Democratic urban communities

Human beings are not totally determined by their environment – indeed they help to construct it. People make their lives and their urban places as much as urban places make the people. They make their own agenda as they walk and talk, interact, and choose and choose not to choose. The big story of our times – the meta-narrative of our post-modernism – is undoubtedly shopping. The global market-place determines so much of how we interact and decide, and this ideology is imposed from above and squeezes us into the urban places it forms. But we can be counter-cultural, revelling in the brighter side of globalization – the multiplicity, the mixity (see Massey 1999) and the differences it brings. In this new meeting place where different cultures, understandings and lifestyles abound, there is place for experimentation, projects, programmes and communities with a mysterious power for human beings at the level of everyday living – and that is where it counts. It is interesting, for example, to see that all across the world there is an expansive upsurge of local Pentecostal groups in the urban areas. They feel fresh and upbeat, empowering and affirming their members. In the UK, those members often have multiple foci – belonging with a deep rootedness in a mother country as well as the new UK culture. This new urban Pentecostalism has, we believe, touched the spring of the powerful cosmopolitan energy at work at the local urban level – an energy both immanent and transcendent, not merely local and global, but local and universal.

In this urban mixity, we are meeting others on this same journey. For example, Leonie Sandercock seems to have got there ahead of us when, as a radical city planner, she tells us that we need to 're-sacralize' the built urban environment, its human communities and ecology (Sandercock 1998). In her view, we can indeed work from the very local level – from below – forming groups committed to analysing our situation and working together to realize our inclusive vision. She offers a method of analysis for such groups which can only really function from below. In addition to the usual 'scientific' ways of knowing, she suggests a method of 'knowing through dialogue; from experience; through seeking out local knowledge of the specific and concrete; through learning to read symbolic, non-verbal evidence; through contemplation; and through action-planning' (Sandercock 2003: 76). We might see this as a challenge to the Church to reclaim its earliest traditions, to rejoin the marginalized on the streets of our towns and cities and to bring the very best of our Spirit-inspired imaginations to a listening and observing style of mission. Urban theologians have described this form of mission in both theoretical and practical detail (see Green 2003) and have challenged the Church to get back in touch with its own traditions of engagement with the underside of society in order that society should be saved from itself – in conformity to the model of mission offered by Jesus himself. The Church must break away from its tendency to create an inward-looking and private 'family' haven in each locality, and engage instead in dialogue with all others of goodwill who see the need for ordinary people to become the subjects of their own history, and no longer merely its objects.

Learning from past experience

Before we reflect on what the Church distinctively has to offer by way of principles and praxis for the good urban community, we should perhaps pause and reflect upon a lesson from history – for this is not the first time that churches have been challenged to engage with new urban areas on the edge of towns and cities. In the 1960s and '70s some members of the Church in the UK thought it had the answers to the new urban areas and that its mission was guaranteed to be a success. History shows that the reality was somewhat different, and that perhaps future enterprises need to reflect on this experience if earlier disillusionments are to be avoided and opportunities are to be grasped.

In the mid-1960s and early '70s, when the New Town building programme was at its height, the New Town Ministers Association (NTMA), a dynamic and well-organized professional network of several hundred ministers from different denominations, assumed that to plan churches for the New Town communities required the simple (but not necessarily simplistic) application of bureaucratic planning techniques based on methods and assumptions directly borrowed from the Development Corporations. These Corporations were the government planning agencies created by an Act of Parliament to deliver the comprehensive master plans, usually over a period of 25 years. They were required to build these new communities from scratch. The apotheosis of the NTMA engagement with the New Town development movement was an intensive residential conference in 1971, in which the delegates were invited to engage in a live planning exercise for a fictitious New Town of 80,000 people called 'Schechem'. The title for the subsequent conference report (NTMA 1971) was *Secular City, New Jerusalem*. This exercise was designed to enable better co-ordination and planning for future New Towns and town extensions, which at the time were assumed to be the default *modus operandi* of government-sponsored urban and community development. The delegates had to decide the fictitious placement and design of churches and the deployment of parish and sector ministers, under the observation of town planners and other consultants who commented and advised on the decision-making process.

Interestingly, this high point in the life of the NTMA and its belief in the power of top-down ecumenical planning was followed swiftly by a sense of disenchantment and failure. The reason was a strong sense of being controlled by the inner group who had planned the essentials of the project and were running the day-to-day processes. It dawned on several delegates what it must feel like to be a resident of an existing community who is told where you can live and what your choices may be – in short, to be disempowered by expert-driven and preconceived solutions to the perceived problems of your old community. There was also a growing recognition that the complexity of human interaction with the built environment not only should not, but could not be reduced to a series of technological plans and statistical charts. Where was the room for failure, spontaneity, the valuing of memory and tradition, for spirituality and ritual? Schechem, it transpired, was not the New Jerusalem – neither the perfect model for the town of the future, nor the perfect model church of the future.

Thirty years on, instead of government-sponsored New Towns delivered by Development Corporations, we have the market equivalent in the Thames Gateway. As we saw in Chapter 4, these 'new towns' and communities will be built from scratch with development monies from investment and pension funds, but without the integrated social and community infrastructure the Development Corporations had as their brief. Nor will these new communities primarily be for families and blue-collar workers, as they were in the twentieth century. These twenty-first-century new urban areas appear in the first instance to be primarily designed for the single or professional couples who will prefer to rent rather than buy. Service workers and low-paid public workers will also have to rent, since the current demand for housing close to London-bound transport hubs will put the price of a starter home beyond their reach.

But also, these new urban areas, and the people that will come to live in them, will be surprisingly diverse and will continue to resist the lure of a single theological blueprint or ecclesiological master plan. As we saw in Chapter 8, the multiplicity of communities within the Thames Gateway has generated a multiplicity of church models to engage with them. There is no 'Schechem' or one-size-fits-all answer to the Thames Gateway. Instead, as we have already intimated, the theological and ecclesiological response will need to be complex, variable, subtle, performative and creative.

A theology of relationships

Our resulting understanding of mission requires that contextual theology no longer be the imposition of pre-formulated theological constructs upon a locality, but a careful praxis of interchange between action, experience and reflection from our traditions. Practical theology which starts at pavement level like this will be like the scraps of bread collected in Galilee after the 5,000 followers had seen a miracle and eaten their fill. The fragments of local pavement-level truth are collected and found to be unsystematic and inevitably provisional and experimental. Urban theology is not written in statements but in relationships – and perhaps this is the only true theology, for truth, the Bible tells us, is a relationship, not a statement. Jesus asks his followers to be in relationship one with another, with him and with his Father, so that the truth will be in them. So it is that relationships in the urban space make the new place, and it is not the new spaces, however grandly drawn by architects or planners, that make community relationships. Indeed, modern urban relationships, as we noted in Chapter 7, may even turn out to be non-spatial – rather like the relationships of the earliest nomadic communities. The letter to the Hebrews tells us that, of all those who truly sought the city of heaven, the most faithful was Abraham the nomad (see Hebrews 11.8–10). Modern anthropologists have noted that Australian Aboriginals define their land not by place but by the journeys they make across it, and these tracks are not lines of division but of connection. We might, with Michael Nausner (Keller, Nausner and Rivera 2004: 127), see, in this nomadic networking, resonances with Jesus' dynamic relationship with the land and his nomadic lifestyle – all this pointing to today's post-modern generation, whose restless mobility may seem on the surface to deny a sense of 'community'. The groups that we join to undertake the looking and listening enjoined by Sandercock's analysis may well prove to be those urban neo-nomads, networking between the watering-holes, using the Web and mobile communication to establish community. It is here in these spaces and at the watering-holes and shrines that the new church must establish new liturgy. As we suggested in Chapter 7, we must learn to 'be with', not only to 'be in'.

A theology of partnerships

The Church is increasingly invited by government and others to become a deliverer of services to the needy. This may sound very fine in itself, but strings are often attached to the invitation. First, receiving money to undertake the care carries obligations to offer the care in the way prescribed by the donor. Notoriously, the Labour government under James Callaghan invited local Community Development Projects to undertake significant urban redevelopment work in the UK's poorest communities. However, as soon as the Projects asked questions, not about how resources could be provided for the poor, but why the poverty existed in the first place, funding was immediately withdrawn and the workers sacked. Becoming an agent of a government which has bought into the neo-liberal mindset carries great dangers for the integrity of the partner. Privatizing welfare is an essential ingredient of the politics of the globalization of neo-liberalism. We are also aware that in much provision of care and urban development programmes, many consultants are making enormous profits and earning exorbitant salaries on the backs of the poor who should be receiving the benefits. As we have argued in Chapter 8, this is not to say that the Church should not form partnerships with other agencies, but that it is important that our own agenda be safeguarded in all our partnering and that in all our work the Church should always ask, 'Who is most benefiting from this programme?' The Church of England was instrumental in the creation of the welfare state in the UK and we and other Christian denominations and faith groups must not be seen to be instrumental in its privatization and demolition.

However, we have already argued for openness and inclusivity, and this means that partnerships will be of the essence of church in the New Jerusalem. We have reminded ourselves that the Christian faith is anything but risk-averse. Our security is not in self-preservation and isolation but in meeting with those who look least likely to be the gateway to heaven, as Jesus did. We must therefore engage forthrightly with the new urban developments and all those who are involved in their planning, development and ongoing management. But we must do so with a firm grip on our own identity as Christians and our own agenda as followers of the Way. This will mean taking our theological reflection always with us into the negotiating chamber. How will this look in practical terms?

First, we must not demonize developers, because within their ranks we will find angels – those who bring messages of hope and renewal for our communities and are fighting with all their skill to see that bright vision fulfilled, knowing full well the strict limits within which they are commanded to operate. So we too must be canny about Section 106 agreements, tight time-frames, and the like, understanding why the developers are having to be mindful of their 'bottom line' – profit. We must appreciate that the situation is new and that we cannot therefore merely act in accordance with our own previous procedures. We have always assumed, for example, that we build human communities first before determining whether or not a building is necessary. The planning procedures in modern developments rarely allow this generosity of time any longer – we cannot play catch-up when all the land is allocated and bought for domestic accommodation, especially when land values are some ten times higher for housing development than for building community facilities. So we must learn the vocabulary of urban development – and, by the way, not be fearful of the professionals, because we will soon learn that our parishioners usually know more about the real community than any of us will ever know. We are not good, however, at knowing how to operate before a local community exists, and to counter this we need plenty of networking so that we may all learn good practice and steer clear of the pitfalls.

A manifesto for the good city

The Church is not a debating chamber, although it is often portrayed as such by the national media, and we can therefore fall into the trap of becoming what they want us to be. The local embodiment of church is often altogether different, however, not for ever turning flesh into words but, in a fully incarnational way, making the word become flesh by manifesting itself in practical, hands-on works of witness. This is not a battle between being and doing, but rather a dynamic of action and reflection as the Church strives to become what it is given to become by its Lord. It is right, therefore, that we should list some of the very practical ways in which the ideas we are delineating here might work out at local parish level. We would therefore argue that, first, the Church should work in practical ways to see community and identity established in our new urban areas, and that, second, space should be made sacred again. It is time to offer some principles by which each of these key contributions to the good city can be inculturated in our new urban spaces.

Establishing community and identity in
new urban areas

We would like to propose five principles by which to establish a renewed sense of community and identity in new urban areas. This process, we believe, is essential if we are to produce sustainable communities in the social as well as the economic and environmental sense.

A first principle of a good city is to learn to enjoy once again what it is to live in urban contested space, getting out of our cocooning cars and gated communities, and cultivating a renewed appetite for meeting the other – in the mixity of cosmopolitan life and in the mystery of eucharist.

A second principle is to create a new theology of societal competition. Sociologists talk of the functional model of society as opposed to the conflictual model, the latter being the negotiation of opposing groups in contested space and the resulting dynamic creating what the society becomes. It is this latter model which resonates with everything we have been discovering in the new urban areas, and all that we learn of the life and death of Jesus as he confronts challenges similar to our own. This sociological understanding will be important as we seek to formulate a practical theology of action for our witness and mission.

Third, we have spoken of a nomadic way of being community and the Church will need to think again about how its parochial model relates to those who adopt this new mobile lifestyle.

Fourth, we recognize the key lesson that church plants simply must address the neighbourhood in which they are planted. So-called 'community churches' are springing up in many of our localities, but many of them have little or no allegiance to the geographical locality and are apt to 'up sticks and move' at any time. We must engage with this phenomenon and learn its lessons. Surely there is a place for rooted space even in a mobile society – after all, who can tell whether such an oil-based culture can be sustainable?

Finally, new communities are growing up everywhere and the Church must be there in their midst. We have spoken of the communities which cluster around social events, niche interests, voluntary gatherings, new tribes and political or leisure pursuits. We have a growing array of retail, sports and event chaplaincies and it is our duty to analyse these more rigorously so that we can learn their strengths and pitfalls.

Making public space sacred again

We now offer some principles by which a sense of the sacred might once again be experienced in our public spaces, as a counterbalance to the increasingly privatized and utilitarian use to which land and the built environment are being put. We work here with a very broad and inclusive sense of the term 'sacred'. We understand the term in ways that resonate with the ideas of Philip Sheldrake (2001). He describes sacred space as any building or public space that causes us to reflect on the ultimate meaning of life – that takes us away from the concerns and preoccupations of the present and causes us to reflect on the values and visions of a good urban space. Sacred spaces are those spaces precious to us, individually or collectively, because in some way we have invested in them something deep within ourselves. Sheldrake is concerned about the apparent disposability of so much contemporary life, which feels so utilitarian and homogenized. Our understanding of 'sacred' is also based on the importance of memory, in that some buildings, spaces and natural monuments hold the collective memory of communities and the history of their shared experience. Our broad definition recognizes the ongoing importance of 'sacred spaces' as traditionally understood – as set aside from the secular, or everyday, concerns of the city. Churches and other religious buildings are still important to core communities, but increasingly are becoming significant also for those still seeking a sense of the spiritual and the numinous but who want to find it in ways and places that offer anonymity and do not threaten personal autonomy. Thus cathedrals have enjoyed a steady increase in the number of visitors and in Sunday attendance over recent years. But Sheldrake is keen to point out, not least in view of some of the strong anti-urban rhetoric within the Judaeo-Christian tradition, that the sacred will be found across a broad spectrum that includes everyday profane space outside the temple as well as those spaces inside the temple. It is in the spirit of this expansive theological principle that we offer the following seven principles.

First, we believe in the importance of reclaiming the streets and open urban places as public. For example, developers are mandated to include open green space in our new urban areas, but many green spaces turn out to be enclosed or behind barriers. Many leisure and shopping areas have been privatized and no longer allow the public free access. God has given us the planet to share for our own health and for the sake of justice, and so we must engage politically and negotiate publicly to make this possible.

Our second principle is to endorse a Trinitarian theology, outlined earlier, that where human beings commune with each other they are true to their creator's image in them as social beings. We must therefore open places up as opportunities for human interaction – no longer just for controlled consumerism, but for shared hobbies, interests and communal celebration. Our church premises are so important in this regard.

Third, we remind the Church of its prophetic vocation, whereby it will often be called upon to stand in the way of new urban developments when they are manifestly not in the human interest. If the poor are to be decanted and ignored, if the environment is to be despoiled simply for financial gain, if developers are not listening to the real needs of local communities, if suburban sprawl is all we are being offered, then it is the Christian duty to speak out against the dominating interests of imperialistic development.

Fourth, we must be ready to work willingly with other specialist groups such as CABE (the Commission for Architecture and the Built Environment) and local-regeneration delivery companies in order to influence building design and public planning strategy toward socially sustainable environments that include a sense of the sacred, or at least allow the development of this in the future.

Fifth, we must work nationally to criticize British regional policy – utilizing our national church base to offer voices from across the North–South spectrum, especially opening up the question of why the South must overheat economically and the North genuflect to the South.

Sixth, we must work hard to bring urban concerns back into a more positive focus within the Church. Despite many church reports and debates, there remains in the Church an antipathy across the board toward investing heavily in personnel, training and finance when it comes to urban ministry and mission. And yet this is where the vast majority of the population live or work. We must also help the Church to understand how the various styles of the urban (suburban, inner city, finance centres and poor estates) are related and how these all impinge upon the rural. If this holistic vision escapes us then we will no longer have a 'Church of England'.

Finally, having appreciated that holistic vision, we must still underscore what is distinctive about urban mission and ministry and train our laity and clergy for it. But the old styles of urban training will not do – it is a new world out there.

Conclusion: to value only what is of true value

The Christian knows, along with many others who seek the Divine, that ultimate value is to be found only in the living God. The mindset lying behind much of the development of our new urban areas believes that value and quality are to be determined by the marketplace. Thus we can be at odds with the underlying forces that determine how our new urban areas are planned, developed and managed. However, the Christian also believes that God is everywhere redeeming creation and that we dare not demonize others lest we ourselves be found equally wanting. Our place is therefore to engage forthrightly, but with ever-increasing sophistication, with the world as followers of him who was in the world for our sake. This incarnation of God in Christ is how we know that matter matters to God and that physical concerns are God's concerns and therefore spiritual matters. God offers us the New Jerusalem in order to rekindle our faith that God's will may be done in an urbanized world as it is in heaven. But as the Church is called upon to respond to a very new globalized and urbanized world, it must adopt some of the new paradigms of mission and ministry identified above in order to proclaim the gospel in this generation. However, as we have seen throughout this book, the new urban areas are highly complex built spaces, and so that proclamation will need to be clear and unambiguous, yet also highly nuanced and contextualized.

The Church has much to offer to the new urban areas and we must not be slow to offer it. We have, for example, a real presence in each urban community. We have been serving most of them since their inception and we have stayed through thick and thin. We have a total commitment, with our clergy legally obliged to live in their parishes, many doing so with their families expressly to experience the joys and sorrows of the community in all their fullness. Add to this the fact that the Church is not only in communion with people of like mind but also working constantly with those who have different backgrounds and reasons for being in these localities – we are the guardians of the stories of many – and it is clear that we seek to provide what is nowadays called 'linking social capital' across the boundaries of the various groups and parties in the community. We not only offer linking capital but can draw upon a vast national and local resource of buildings and volunteers with wide and timely experience. Above all else, the Church comes to the urban areas with a wealth of spiritual resources – prayer, Bible, sacrament, worship and the gifts of the Spirit.

With all this to offer, the Church should not be afraid of engaging with the challenges of the new urban areas. Despite the immense creativity and innovation produced by global flows, which offer the opportunity to millions to move on and create a new sense of identity and begin a new life, we have nevertheless also observed that these new opportunities and dynamics need to be grounded in order to mitigate their worst imbalances. We have seen these imbalances of space and opportunity polarize new and existing communities and disfigure the sense of collective responsibility and experience so necessary for creating sustainable communities. But it is important to remember that the Church's resources are not only physical, but just as important, value-based and ethically motivated. In the language of capital, we not only have religious capital to offer, in the form of buildings, partnerships, personnel and investment, but also spiritual capital – our values, visions and theological identity which bring an ultimate, transcendent perspective to bear on a vision of human happiness that often seems horribly short-term and expedient. These are counter-cultural values and often appear to fly in the face of prevailing economic and development wisdom.

These counter-cultural values are vital if we are to challenge the shallow Utopianism inherent in the rhetoric and design values surrounding the Thames Gateway. The New Jerusalem – the city free from pain and suffering in which the nations of the world are healed and reconciled – is only reached through a journey of engagement with the cross and the experiences of crucifixion. The cross stands as a symbol of multi-dimensional reconciliation between people and

God, people and each other, and the whole created order. The cross stands as a symbol of reconciliation in both the present and the future (see Atherton 2000). The Church has the tools to face the exciting challenges of our new urban areas – however insignificant we may feel and even though we offer values that are against the grain. But the crucifixion was just such an act of powerlessness 'against the grain', and yet it was that which ushered in the New Jerusalem.

References

Atherton, J., *Public Theology for Changing Times*. SPCK, London, 2000.

Boff, L., 'A Theological Response to Ecological Crisis', *Voices from the Third World*, 16(1).

Davey, A. P., 'Better Place: Performing the Urbanisms of Hope', *International Journal of Public Theology*, 2 (2008): 27–46.

Green, L., *Urban Mission and the Kingdom of God*. SPCK, London, 2003.

Keller, C., Nausner, M., and Rivera, M., *Postcolonial Theologies: Divinity and Empire*. Chalice Press, St Louis, Mo., 2004.

Massey, D., *World City*. Polity Press, Cambridge, 2007.

Massey, D., Allen, J., and Pile, S. (eds), *City Worlds*. Routledge, London, 1999.

NTMA (New Town Ministers Association), *Secular City, New Jerusalem. The Report of the Conference on Planning for Mission: Bulletin No. 4*. New Town Ministers Association, London, 1971.

ODPM (Office of the Deputy Prime Minister), *Sustainable Communities: Building for the Future*. ODPM, Wetherby, 2003.

Sandercock, L., *Cosmopolis II: Mongrel Cities in the 21st Century*. Continuum, London, 2003.

Sandercock, L., *Towards Cosmopolis: Planning for Multicultural Cities*. John Wiley, Chichester, 1998.

Shah, H., and Marks, N., *A Well-Being Manifesto for a Flourishing Society*. New Economics Forum, London, 2004.

Sheldrake, P. F., *Places for the Sacred: Place, Memory and Identity*. SCM Press, London, 2001.

Ward, G., *Cities of God*. Routledge, London, 2000.

Index of biblical references

Index of subjects